Sharp Edges

Knives in America's History

C. J. Vannoy

HERITAGE BOOKS
2009

HERITAGE BOOKS
AN IMPRINT OF HERITAGE BOOKS, INC.

Books, CDs, and more—Worldwide

For our listing of thousands of titles see our website at
www.HeritageBooks.com

Published 2009 by
HERITAGE BOOKS, INC.
Publishing Division
100 Railroad Ave. #104
Westminster, Maryland 21157

Copyright © 2009 Cynthia Vannoy-Rhoades

All rights reserved. No part of this book may be reproduced or transmitted in any form or by any means, electronic or mechanical, including photocopying, recording or by any information storage and retrieval system without written permission from the author, except for the inclusion of brief quotations in a review.

International Standard Book Numbers
Paperbound: 978-0-7884-4556-9
Clothbound: 978-0-7884-8155-0

Sharp Edges

Table of Contents

Sharp Edges: Knives in America's History

1. Knives of the Indians	page 1
2. Knives of the Explorers	page 14
3. Knives of the Westward Expansion	page 25
4. Knives of the Revolutionary War	page 37
5. Knives of the Mountain Men	page 50
6. Knives of the Buffalo Skinners	page 61
7. Knives of the Gold Fields	page 70
8. Knives of the Civil War	page 81
9. Knives of the Plains Cavalry	page 94
10. Knives of the Trail Hands	page 106
11. Knives of the Gamblers	page 116
Afterword	page 125
Footnotes	page 126
Bibliography	page 133

Vannoy

List of Illustrations

Page   5 – An Obsidian Knife Blade
Page   7 – Two Arrowheads
Page 13 – Arrowheads and Chippings
Page 15 – Viking Dagger
Page 17 – Rondel Dagger
Page 20 – Viking Sword
Page 24 – Castillo de San Marcos
Page 26 – Trade Knives
Page 28 – Folding Knives
Page 33 – Indian Knife
Page 36 – Modern Bowie
Page 38 – Guardless Bowie Knife
Page 40 – Patch Knife
Page 44 – Measuring Knife and Spontoon Head
Page 47 – Pen Knife
Page 52 – Green River Skinning Knife
Page 55 – Butcher Knife
Page 58 – Modern Tomahawk
Page 64 – Buffalo Skinning Knife, Green River Skinner
Page 67 – Butcher Knife & Bowie
Page 72 – Butcher Knife
Page 77 – Butcher Knife
Page 82 – Confederate Bowie Knife
Page 96 – Pocket Knife
Page 102 – General Custer with Sword
Page 108 – Cowboy with Knife
Page 112 – Modern Three-Blade Pocket Knife
Page 114 – Modern Barlow
Page 118 – Push Dagger
Page 122 – Boot Knife

Vannoy

Preface and Acknowledgements

The following chapters appeared in *Blade Magazine* in shorter form: November/December 1986, *Buffalo Skinner Knives*; March/April 1987, *Knives of the Cowboys*; July/August 1987, *Knives of the Indians*; September/October 1988, *Knives of the Gamblers*; November/December 1987, *Knives of the Mountain Men*; and May/June 1988, *Knives of the Frontier Cavalry*.

Foreword

Knives have fired the imagination of people for centuries. They were the first weapons to be developed, and have been used in warfare since the first man discovered he could kill an enemy with a knife easier than pitching rocks at him. Indians made knives of stone or bone, more advanced civilizations made them of metal, working it into sharp, cutting edges and ornate hilts.

Knives have been tools, weapons, decorations, presentation pieces, collector's items, and the badge of manhood. Few pioneer boys were considered men unless they had a pocketknife, usually a Barlow. A soldier felt naked on a campaign without a knife of some sort, and a cowboy would often be lost without his trusty knife. Explorers, settlers, gamblers, and gold miners used knives, and the Bowie knife made history for its owner, and it is probably the only knife to actually go down in history.

Most others, the Green River Skinners, the I. Wilson knives, the Dadley, the Barlow, the Arkansas Toothpick, the push dagger and others, are only of interest to collectors, but nearly everyone has heard of the famous Bowie knife, and its owner, Jim Bowie. For this reason, I have chosen to only mention the Bowie in a limited way, although it was impossible not to give considerable space to it, as it crossed many cultures; was used by many different levels of society and has been copied more than any other style of knife.

This book is not designed to be a collector's guide to knives, we have several good ones and I didn't have that in mind at the start. What I wanted to do was to find old references that showed how important knives were to the various people in our history, and what kind of knives were popular during the various time frames I have included. I only went as far as the turn of the century, as the knives were more important before the rifles and pistols were refined.

Vannoy

I am sure readers will find some I have missed, or should have included. I hope they will forgive me.

Chapter 1
Indian Knives

Before the coming of the Europeans, the Indians on the North American Continent were skilled craftsmen, living off the land and fashioning tools and weapons from the materials that nature offered, bone, rock, antler, ivory, or wood. Seacoast tribes often used shark's teeth for small, serrated knives, and sharpened clamshells and the shoulder blades of large turtles to make edged tools.

Metal was not wildly used until the coming of the white men. However, there were some exceptions. The Old Copper people, who lived near the Great Lakes region from about 5000 B.C. until 500 B.C., discovered that the copper ore lying near the surface of the earth made great tools and pounded it into knife blades. Nearly 1,000 years later, the Hopewell Indians, and some Northern tribes, revived the art.

Copper tools have been found in New York and Florida and on the Great Plains, evidence of a healthy trade economy flourishing in the early days. What copper the Indians used was pure copper, found in small deposits near the earth's surface. Pure copper is relatively soft and brittle, although it can be hardened considerably by pounding it cold. The Indians sharpened the edges by careful hammering after they shaped the knife. Still, the blades had to be wide and thick to prevent breaking and crumbling. Because of this, the usual shape for a copper dagger blade was a short, broad triangle. Handles were wood, bone or ivory.

Most tribes didn't live near copper deposits, so the favored material for weapons and tools was rock. Rock was easy to find, a lot of it, and the right kind of rock worked nicely into knives, arrowheads, and other tools.

What type of rock was used depended upon two major

Sharp Edges

factors: How easy it was to come by and how easily it worked into tools. Some rock was too brittle, too hard, or too soft to make good knives. Flint, given the fact that it is widespread throughout North America, was probably the most widely used tool making material. It flaked easily, was hard enough to make lasting tools and was fairly easy to find.

In areas of prehistoric volcanic activity, obsidian is often found. Obsidian was the favored the rock for tool making among the Indian tribes living near deposits of the volcanic glass. Obsidian, a hard, brittle glass formed when hot lava cooled very quickly, was the optimum knife making material. It chipped easily, is very hard, and very, very sharp. In fact, a single flake spalled from a large chunk of obsidian offers an edge 500 times sharper than surgical steel. Modern day surgeons occasionally use obsidian scalpels for delicate operations, such as eye surgery. Surgeons who have used obsidian scalpels say that they make a cleaner wound than metal, cutting rather than tearing the flesh.

The Indian, of course, didn't know or care about all this modern technology. They just knew that it worked for what they wanted it to do. Obsidian Cliff, in what is now Yellowstone National Park, is a cache of obsidian, and was a favored spot by area tribes for obtaining the black glass. Yearly treks were made to Yellowstone for the purpose of obtaining obsidian, both for use in the tribe, and for trade purposes. In the book, *The History of Archery,* it comments on the use of flint and obsidian for tools and arrowheads, "Thus flint and obsidian arrowheads would be found not only in those areas where the stones occur, but in regions where the stones could be obtained by barter or through seizure of a source of supply. Deposits where flint was easily obtained were often the subject of constant conflict as tribe after tribe endeavored to seize and retain use of these valuable holdings."[1]

Obsidian from the Yellowstone deposits has been found in burial mounds of the Hopewell Indians, who lived throughout Illinois, Ohio, and New York.

Making tools from stone required a lot of time, and skill. Very often, the tribe had a man who was exceptionally skilled at the task who made most of the tribe's knives, arrowheads and other stone tools, although nearly every warrior could and did fashion his weapons and tools as necessary.

In the book, *Hunting with a Bow and Arrow*, Saxton Pope describes how Ishi, the last Yaha Indian in California, made and arrowhead out of obsidian. Ishi, found nearly starved near Deer Creek, California, in 1911, was the only survivor of a nearly stone age race of people that were thought to have been extinct, or at least rounded up and put on a reservation, in 1872. Ishi was turned over to Professor T.T. Watterman, Department of Anthropology at the University of California. Watterman, after establishing a common language, a nearly forgotten Indian dialect that Ishi could understand, took Ishi to the Museum of Anthropology in San Francisco, where he met Dr. Pope, and lived for five years as a living museum exhibit, giving us an insight into the life of primitive American peoples.

In making stone tools, such as knives and arrowheads, Ishi, "began this work by taking one chunk of obsidian and throwing it against another; several small pieces were thus shattered off. One of these, approximately three inches long, two inches wide, and a half an inch thick, was selected as suitable for an arrowhead, or *haka*. Protecting the palm of his left hand by a piece of thick buckskin, Ishi placed a piece of obsidian flat upon it holding it firmly with his fingers folded over it.

"In his right hand he held a short stick on the end of which was lashed a sharp piece of deer horn. Grasping the horn firmly while the longer extremity lay beneath his forearm, he pressed the point of the horn against the edge of the obsidian. Without jar or blow, a flake of glass flew off, as large as a fish scale. Repeating this process at various spots on the intended head, turning it from side to side, first reducing one face, than the other, he soon had a symmetrical point. In half and hour he could make the most graceful and perfectly proportioned arrowheads imaginable." 2

Various tribes, depending on their culture, used specialized knives and the uses they put their knives to. The Chipewyan Indians of Upper Alberta, Canada, used copper, bone and stone knives to skin and flesh caribou hides to be used for clothing. Often, a caribou leg, broken across to provide an oval cutting edge, was used to scrape the meat off the hide. After the hide was dried, it was scraped with a small, hoe-shaped copper blade on an antler handle. The men also used a crooked knife, with a very thin blade crooked or curled at the

Sharp Edges
end of the blade, with a wooden handle. Blades could be made of copper, or reworked metal. The copper used for the blade was nearly pure, pounded into shape, and hammered to a sharp edge. The Chipewyan also knew the technique of honing a blade on a stone to keep it sharp. Later, these crooked knives were a staple in the Indian trade, with the earliest example being 1806, when Auguste Chouteau, one of the founders of the Missouri fur trade, was billed by Hunt and Hankison, jobbers, for "crooked knives" at $.25 each. These were usually shipped blade only, and the Indians fitted the on the handles they desired.

Eskimo's in Arctic lands, both in Greenland and in North America, used an ulu, which seems to have developed only in arctic countries, possibly brought from the Old World during the ice age. The ulu is an unusual knife, with the blade being a semi-circular, half-moon shape with the handle attached to the top of the blade. The blades have been made out of slate or metal, and the handles made of wood or bone. It was considered a woman's tool, used for cutting leather for clothing, scraping hair and blubber off hides, and cutting meat for the stew pot.

Knives evolved as they were needed within certain cultures. No culture shows this more clearly than the arctic cultures.
Besides the ulu, people of the far north developed the "snow-knife", a long-bladed knife made of either bone or antler,
used to cut blocks of wind-packed snow to quickly construct the round, dome shaped igloo, that could be heated with body heat and a stone lamp.
Knives were mostly tools, but some were also used in ceremonies. One such knife was a story knife, made by Eskimos. The story knife was often a beautiful piece of work, carved from ivory, and decorated with elaborate drawings, it was used by the story tellers of the tribe to sketch scenes from his tales in the snow, to while away the long Arctic nights.
Another ceremonial knife was the bear knife, a sacred object of the Blackfoot tribes. "The Blackfoot tribes possessed several bear-knife bundles, and their owners carried these to war to be employed in battle. The bear knife was a splendid creation, usually of the stabber type with a huge, broad, double-edged blade and with either a large flat wooden handle or one made from a bear's jaw with the teeth

Vannoy

An obsidian knife blade, courtesy of Crazy Crow Trading Company, Pottsboro, TX .

Sharp Edges

remaining. The bundles were subject to purchase and were passed on with traditional ceremonies." 3

Knives were occasionally used in warfare. Northwest coast Indians made stabbing daggers out of wood, as did the Mandans in present day North Dakota. Four Bears, the Mandan Chief that George Catlin visited with and painted, wore a wooden knife, which, as Catlin put it, "had seen bloodshed."

The Pueblo Indians were using stone knives for scalpers in Coronado's time, and in the writings of Genaro Garcia, who accompanied Cortez into Mexico, he says of Indians encountered there, "...and they attacked us hand to hand, some with lances, some shooting arrows, and others with two handed knife-edged swords..." the authors footnote says these were macuahuitls, or wooden sword edged with sharp flint or obsidian. *4* However, it wasn't until the Europeans introduced metal blades that knives were used to any extent in warfare, and then only as a last resort.

Four Bears recounted this bloody tale to George Catlin, illustrating the use of a knife. Borrowing Catlin's watercolors, the chief did a painting illustrating his retelling of a fight between him self and another chief. The two Indians had cast their guns aside, and, when the other chief lunged a Four Bears with his knife, Four Bears parried the stroke by grabbing the blade with his left hand, going for his battle-ax with his right.

For long centuries, Indians lived and warred with other tribes using only weapons formed from what nature gave them, copper, stone, volcanic glass, bone, antler, teeth and shell. With the coming of the Europeans, the Indian way of life changed, new tools and weapons began to appear within the tribes, guns, metal knifes, and other items that made life easier, if more dependent on a supply source. Bone, ivory, rock and shell tools began to lose favor and metal began to take their place. Now, only a few enterprising companies, who make obsidian knives, and old arrowheads and knife blades, often found by accident, are all that remain of the cultures that learned to make the best of what was available.

Although Columbus and the Vikings were the first to reach the New World, they didn't carry on extensive trade with the tribes. Columbus took a few natives back to show the civilized world, and the Vikings may have captured a few as well, but it wasn't until the

Two fine arrowheads from the author's collection, the one on the right is a Sioux Arrowhead and the one on the left was found near Clearmont, Wyoming, origin unknown. Both show the fine craftsmanship of an artist at his trade.

Sharp Edges
1500's, with the Spanish exploration of Mexico and the Southwestern U.S. that trade between the Indian tribes and the Europeans became extensive.

In 1583, Espejo's expedition found no metal weapons or horses among the tribes of what is now Texas, but 100 years later the Jumanos Indians in the Northern Rio Grande country were busy trading Spanish goods, such as horses and knives, to the Caddoan Indians in East Texas.

The Spanish took advantage of the trading fairs, such as the one in Taos described in 1780. This fair, "grew into a major regional occasion. Each August, wrote a Spanish Chronicler, the Indians arrive in Taos with "pieces of chamois, many buffalo skins, and, out of plunder they obtained elsewhere, horses, muskets, munitiions, knives, meat." 5   These fairs had been going on for centuries, the tribes coming together peacefully to exchange goods. Northern tribes bought dried meat and fish; Southern tribes contributed maize and other grains. Both Northern and Southern tribes contributed slaves.

With the introduction of the Spanish goods, the trading fairs increased their commodities. Muskets, metal knives, hatchets, and horses were exchanged for things the Indians had easy access to - slaves and gold. Other than occasionally being used in ceremonies or jewelry, the Indians had little use for gold, it was too soft to be worked into knives, and slaves were easily stolen from other tribes. In exchange, the white men's metal was sharper, and tougher than the Indians rock tools. Knives could be put to use the way they were, or reworked to suit the user. Lances and swords could be cut to size, and used for arrow points or lance points. Axes had many uses, and guns killed quickly and easily. Trade flourished.

Like any group of warring peoples who suddenly find themselves better equipped for war than their fellows, they take advantage of the situation. So it was with several tribes in the American Southwest. Finding that Spanish horses and Spanish weapons were superior to the stone weapons the other tribes used, they began preying on the lesser-equipped tribes. For a time, inequality reigned, until the prosecuted tribes began to acquire the better weapons, and the balance was restored.

The tribes not only preyed on other Indians. Armed with better weapons and losing their awe of the Spaniards, they began to

Vannoy

kill white men as well. The Spanish, seeing the threat posed by the Indians, began passing laws restricting trade.

In 1726, a law was passed prohibiting trading firearms to Indians, and in 1737 a law was passed to prohibit trade with "wild Indians", probably because the Indians had began to prey on the Spanish settlements. This may have helped to keep the weapons out of Indian hands, but not much. Stealing was almost as easy as trading, and the thief was held in higher regard within the tribe than was the trader.

Trade came later to the North. The French and English also traded with the Indian tribes. Knives, axes, guns, blankets, etc., were traded, not for gold and slaves, but for "soft gold", or furs. During the 1700's, the Hudson Bay Company shipped in, among other commodities, twelve gross of French butcher knives, and about 600 hatchets, to be used for trade.

Two knives that were often seen in the Indian trade were dags, and Hudson Bay knives. Dags had broad, stabber-type blades, and were usually sold without a handle, as the Indians preferred to fashion their own handles. This type was often seen among the northwest Coast tribes with handles or with holes drilled in the tang, so the Indians could attach the dag to a thong and wear it around their necks or wrists. In 1824, Governor George Simpson of the Hudson Bay Company passed down the Columbia River, and commented on these dags. "which hung by a thong to the wrist of nearly every male." These came primarily from British trade, via Canada and the Hudson Bay Company. 6

The Hudson Bay Knife was another of British origin. These are long bladed, butcher type knives, similar in type to knives crafted by Indians in the far North for building icehouses, which were dubbed Hudson Bay Knives. Many of these came into Canada during the fur trade days. The Hudson Bay Knife, imported for trade as well as for use by the Hudson Bay employees, has a blade about 8 1/2 inches long, with a three to four inch handle.

In the Eastern U.S., much of the trade was in tableware, rather than spears or butcher knives, and a great many common table knives found their way into Indian camps, and these were sharpened and used as tools. One reference to the Pilgrims mentions knives as trade articles, although it doesn't say what kind of knives were traded.

Sharp Edges

When Lewis and Clark made their trip west to scout the new land purchase, they took several knives along as trade goods to insure friendly relations with the tribes along the way. They saw some evidence of trade among the tribes, mostly good derived from the Spanish settlements to the South. Lewis writes of the Shoshone tribe on August 23rd, 1805, "The metal which we found in possession of these people consisted of a few indifferent knives, a few brass kettles, some arm bands of brass and iron, a few buttons.... a spear or two of a foot in length, and some iron and brass arrow points which they informed me they obtained in exchange for horses from the Crow or Rocky Mountain Indians on the Yellowstone River. The bridle bits and stirrups they obtained from the Spaniards, tho these were but few." 7

On August 24 Lewis writes: "As the Indians who were on their way down the Missouri had a number of spare horses with them I thought it probable I could obtain some of them...I now produced some battle axes which I had made at Fort Mandan with which they were much pleased. knives also seemd in great demand among them. I soon purchased three horses and a mule. for each horse I gave an ax a knife handkerchief and a little paint; & for the mule the addition of a knife a shirt handkerchief and a pair of legings;" 8

The only one that is known to have survived is one in the Lewis and Clark Memorial in Fort Clatsop, Oregon. It is a stag handled dagger that was acquired by the Nez Pence, and was recently passed on to a white person. This knife was the one Clark wrote about on Oct. 5th, 1805, "To each of these three Indians, one of them the son of a chief, I gave a knife." 9

At first, knives were traded here and there, to insure good relations with the tribes, or gain slaves or gold. Later, early in the 1800's, trading knives became big business, and manufacturers began making knives specifically for trade.

It is interesting how the trade differed between the Canadian companies and their American counterparts. In Canada, the Hudson Bay Company treated the Indians as employees, paying them so much in trade for the furs they produced. In this way, they could make use of the Indians skills to collect the furs. In the U.S., the white men did a lot of the trapping, and the Indians brought their furs into the trading posts or rendezvous more like free traders, rather than employees.

Vannoy

In the U.S., the usual trade style knives were "butchers" and "scalpers". Butcher knives were just large, kitchen type butcher knives, usually around 8-10 inches in length. The word, "scalper," or "scalping knife", conjures up images of a deadly-looking, bloody knife, carried by the braves for one purpose, collecting an enemies scalp. Actually, the word "scalper" was coined by the white men, and came to mean any knife that was used mainly in the Indian trade, or the type of knife the Indians preferred to trade for. Indians didn't single out a certain knife or a certain style of knife for scalping. Any knife would work, and work well.

Nearly any knives were traded, examples of butcher knives, hunting style knives, and even sharpened table knives have been seen at Indian sites, reworked barrel hoops, brass kettles, and tiny ink erasers, small, sharp pointed knives, used to make arrowheads, have also been found. About the only style that wasn't popular with the Indians were folders. Indians were hard on their knives, and folders weren't as durable as fixed blades. There was also the problem of the folder closing on the users fingers, and the Indians didn't like to have to worry about being maimed by their own knives. If an Indian did acquire a folder, he usually reworked it so the blade would remain fixed.

No matter where the Indian obtained the knife, he usually ground it down and beveled it on one side only, to be more proficient for skinning chores. Up until around 1836, when J.R. Russell and Company began marketing trade knives, the Indians preferred the English made blades for their knives, and could tell them by the G.R., standing for King George, on the blade. It seems that most American makers marketed cheap knives for trade, trying to get the most for their dollars. The English made knives were of better quality.

In 1832, George Catlin, frontier artist that gained fame for his portraits of Indians, wrote of these trade knives. "The scalping knives and tomahawks are of civilized manufacture, made expressly for Indian use, and carried into Indian country by the thousands and tens of thousands, and sold at an enormous price. The scabbards of the knives and the handles of the tomahawks the Indians construct themselves, according to their own tastes, and oftentimes ornament them very handsomely. In his rude and unapproached condition, the Indian is a stranger to such weapons as these, he works not in metals;

Sharp Edges
and his untutored mind was not ingenious enough to design or execute anything so "savage" or destructive as these civilized "refinements" on Indian barbarity." 10

Trade knives were big business in 1835-1840, during the height of the fur trade.

Records from the American Fur Company, preserved on microfilm, show the volume of trade that went on during these years.

1835: April 24. (Ramsay Crooks, American Fur Company, New York, to Colonel Henry Stanton, Washington, DC, submitting his bid to supply Indian goods to be delivered at Indian treaty grounds, Chicago, August 15, 1835.) Agreeable to your advertisement of 25th ult. 700 scalping knives like sample No. 1 at $.18 each; 700 scalping knives like sample no. 2 at $.15 each. If it is impractical for us to obtain the whole 700 of the No. 1 scalping knives, the deficit will be made up with the No. 2 description at the lower price. The company was awarded the contract.

1840. Feb. 19. Memorandum of sundry goods to be furnished by Hiram Cutler, Sheffield, England, to American Fur Company, N.Y. 60 doz. warranted scalping knives, @ $10.75. (Approximately $.9 each.) There was a slight markup between the price paid by the AFC, and the price they quoted to the government. 11

No matter whether the Indian knives were stone, bone, copper or good English metal, these knives were important to the Indian culture. They were used for war, for work, for ceremonies, and for worship. What tales these broken blades and rusty knives could tell if they could talk.

Some arrowheads and chippings from the author's collection. The red colored one has been broken, and appears to be either a scraper or a knife point, and the brown one on the far right is an arrowhead, but the nocks have broken off.

Sharp Edges

Chapter 2
Knives of the Explorers

Probably the first white people to reach the shores of North America were the Vikings, as early as 1000 A.D. These were the Norseman, rough sailors, looking for plunder or land. With the Vikings probably came the first steel knives and swords to North America.

One of these was the scramasax, the all-purpose knife of the Northmen, Germans, the Franks, and the Anglo-Saxons. According to Harold Peterson, in Daggers and Fighting Knives, he says that the word, Scramasax is of indeterminate meaning. " A sax seems to have been a sword, possibly a single edged sword. The prefix, Scrama might have meant "wound maker", but even this is unclear." Still, it is the name used to refer to these large knives.

"In this context the scramasax was an imposing weapon as well as a general purpose knife. Their blades varied in length from as little as 4 inches to as large as 20 or more inches, when they became in reality short swords. All were single edged and triangular in cross-section with a generally even taper from back to edge." 1 Hilts were usually of wood or bone, and the scramasax had no guards.

"The scramasax was a sturdy knife. The blades were comparatively broad, suitable for dealing a heavy blow in fighting." 2
"Its stout, singled-edged blade, triangular in cross section, could thrust or cut equally well; it could defend its owner against man or beast, could skin and joint game, or cut wood; and it could be used as an eating knife if necessary." 3. Some scramasax blades, like the one attributed to Charlemagne, looks a great deal like a modern Bowie, with the upswept blade and clip point.

Many of these were "pattern welded" more commonly known as Damascus, where several layers of steel are heated together,

Vannoy

A traditional Viking Dagger. ("Photo used with permission, Real Armor of God.com")

Sharp Edges
pounded flat, then bent and reheated, and pounded flat again. This process is repeated until there are up to 300 layers of steel. This forms a blade that is stronger and cuts better than just a pounded piece of steel, and makes unique patterns in the steel. Many Viking knives were highly decorated, as was the case in 1103, when Magnus, King of Norway, went on a colonizing expedition to Ireland. He carried a sword with walrus ivory grips and the metal part of the hilt covered in gold. Other blades have been found with silver and copper plated hilts.

According to Bernard Levine, "The sax was the belt knife and short sword of the Germanic tribes in the Dark Ages, and later of the Vikings." 4

Scramasaxes were highly prized, and, it is said, never left their owner's side, day or night. They were usually buried with the owner at his death. These huge knives were the first to reach the shores of North America.

The Vikings made little mark on America, except for a few legends, a few scattered weapons, and the remains of a village or two in Eastern Canada. A more lasting impression came during the 1500's, when the Spanish explorers, looking for land for the "Country, God, and Gold, landed their galleons on the shores of North America near Florida, and on the shores of Mexico and South America. The Spanish favored swords and muskets. They also carried a variety of daggers.

Although written references to knives are hard to find, because the dagger was a common tool, old drawings show a variety of daggers. Several were common in Spain at the time, and the Conquistadors would have carried the popular models. In American Knives, Harold L. Peterson writes that the popular daggers in Spain at the time were the eared dagger, the rondel dagger, and several versions of the quillon dagger.

The eared dagger was designed with two discs that flared out from either side of the pommel, those made after 1550 form almost a straight line perpendicular to the grips. The grips were formed from the thick tang of blade and covered with such materials as bone, ivory, horn, metal, or wood. These daggers had no guard, but often between the blade and the grips was a spool shaped piece of metal, often damascened in gold. Blades of these daggers were usually

Vannoy

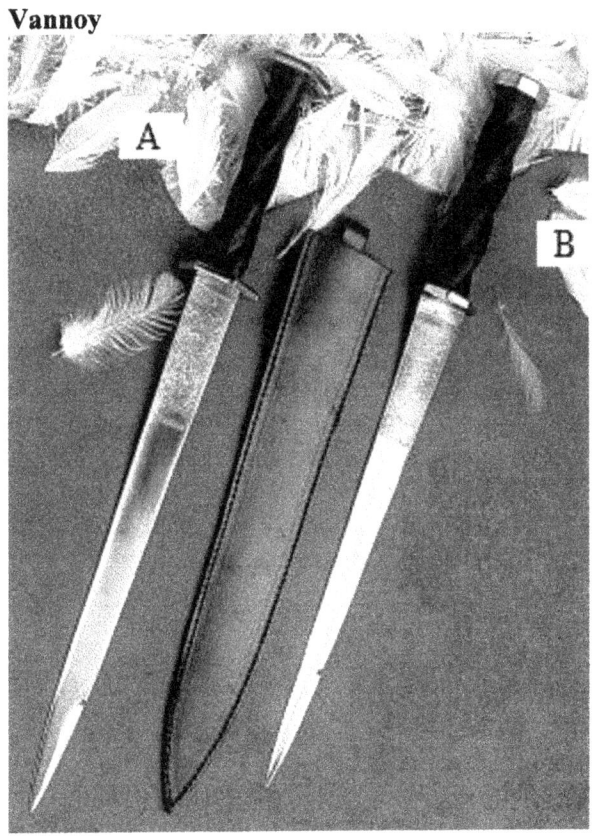

A Rondel Dagger. Variations have been used by many cultures, including the Vikings. ("Photo used with permission, Real Armor of God.com")

Sharp Edges

double edged, with a pronounced ricasso next to the hilt, often longer on one edge than the other. These were carried in a sheath or thrust through the owner's belt. At times it was worn attached to a purse worn on the right of the belt.

More widely used was the rondel dagger, usually a simple dagger, carried by common soldiers, with a double edged blade and a simple grip usually made out of wood, with a two flat discs, or rondels, forming a pommel and a guard. This weapon's main function was to thrust at the enemy, so the point was usually strong.

The third type of dagger was the quillon, with the cross-guard or quillon, which made it resemble a small sword.
This was probably the most widely used knife of the era. The principal function of the guard was to keep the hand from slipping down the blade.

Pommels of these daggers could be in any number of shapes, mushroom, spherical, or fishtail. The grips were usually wood, often carved to give a better grip. Blades could be single edged, double edged, straight or curved.

These early daggers were not fighting knives in the strict sense of the word; their main used being offense, thrusting or stabbing. In journals from the Cortes expedition into Mexico, and the subsequent flight out of Mexico, when the Mexicans, as they called them, revolted in 1520, the writer Genaro Garcia, writes, "Oh, what a sight it was to see this fearful and destructive battle, how we moved all mixed up with them foot to foot, and the cuts and thrusts we gave them, and with what fury the dogs fought..." 5 It wasn't until around 1535 that people began to see the knife as a fighting tool, rather than just a last resort.

Most early users of knife for defense held the knife blade downward, for stabbing and thrusting, rather than the blade up for parrying. George Silver, the famous English swordsman, wrote describing the theory of motion, combined with swift thrusts at the opponent. Before that, fighting had been mostly a matter of two people, standing still and stabbing at each other, trying to penetrate the others armor.

As people began to use Silver's method of fighting, knives changed, the quillons were lengthened to protect the hand, and often curved forward along the blade. Added protection could be created

Vannoy
by rings or an anneau added to the quillon.

These new knives were designed for left-handed use to complement the swordsman, and give him an extra measure of protection. They were normally double edged. In the Hollywood production, The Four Musketeers, one of the musketeers is shown fighting the Cardinal Richelieu, who is using a sword and a left-handed dagger.

But back to America. The Spanish weren't the only explorers interested in the New World. When the French explorers founded a colony, which they named Fort Caroline, near the present day Jacksonville Florida in 1564, they carried quillon daggers. Two old prints by artist Jacques Le Moyne show two ways of wearing the new weapon.

Some thirty years later, when Don Luis de Velasco, a Spaniard who accompanied an expedition into New Mexico wrote that he had, "a sword and a gilded dagger with their waists stitched with purple, yellow, and white silk." 6

As these daggers were most often used in combination with a rapier, they often were made en suite, with the rapier, the decoration of the knuckle guard paralleling that of the cup of the rapier.
One of these daggers is in the Metropolitan Museum of Art, and was featured in a photograph by Paulus Lesser in the Time-Life Book, The Spanish West, page 45. This dagger is a quillon dagger, and is almost identical to the daggers used by the French in Florida, as illustrated in the old prints by Le Moyne from 1564. It has a very ornate pommel and quillon, and looks as if the blade is engraved or damascened.

A rather bloody story concerning knives happened in the New World in 1565, when a Spaniard named Pedro Menendez was ordered to attack the French fort, Caroline, in what is present day Florida. The reason for this was that several Frenchmen, who ran from the new fort after accusing their leader, Laudonniere of lying to them, and luring them to this isolated place with promises of gold. These rebel French men stole a ship and became pirates, until the Spanish caught and hanged them, and King Philip of Spain wanted to make sure that there was no more trouble from Fort Caroline.

He first attacked the fort, in the early dawn. "The scouts closed in on a French sentry and stabbed him." Then Menendez He first attacked the fort, in the early dawn. "The scouts closed in on a

Sharp Edges

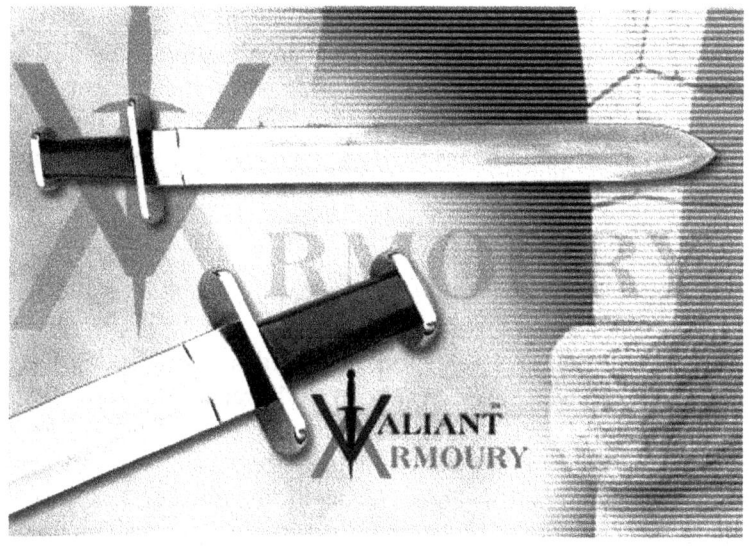

A Viking Sword. ("Photo used with permission, Real Armor of God.com")

Vannoy
French sentry and stabbed him." Then Menendez ordered the charge. The French, still in nightshirts, stumbled out, but the Spaniards, "thrust pike and sword thorough 132 of them." He spared 60. 7

Another load of French were scheduled to appear at the Fort, and they were at the time a hundred miles to the North. Awaiting the ship, Menendez and his soldiers walked the shore in French uniforms, until Ribault, the French commander, came ashore. He told them the fort had fallen, and gave them a choice of risking the Indians, or giving themselves up to the Spanish.

Half the men gave themselves up, the rest stole away towards Canaveral. Menendez and his officers led the French out of sight behind some sand dunes, and drew a line in the sand. He ordered his men, "When the Frenchmen reach this line, cut them down. Knives, swords, and pikes sliced through 134 men." They re-named it San Mateo. 8

The Spanish did no better than the French, after three years of fighting hurricanes, Indian snipers, mosquitoes and other problems; the Spanish were "ruined, aged, weary and full of sickness." 10

Sometime later, the French returned the favor and "shot, stabbed or hanged all 380 Spaniards at the fort...." 11. However, the mosquitoes, hurricanes and Indians were as hard on the French as the Spanish, and they too eventually moved on to the North.

The Spanish found a home in the Southwest. They established a few colonies in California and the Southwest, fighting only Indians. Cortes, Hermosa, Coronado and others explored the Western lands as early a 1519, when Cortes came into Mexico, and left their mark on the culture there. Coronado toured the Southwestern part of the U.S. in 1540, coming as far North as Kansas. (Some historians dispute this, and feel that some of these explorers were as far North as central Wyoming.)
England also wanted a try at the New World, and on Dec. 21, 1620, the Mayflower landed on the shores of Massachusetts, filled with people who came to the New World with a dream.

Being they were some years later than the Spanish and French, the styles of knives had changed again, and the English carried kidney daggers, small single or double-edged blades, with pommels that had two globulra swellings at the base of the grips to prevent the hands from sliding down the knife. These were worn in

Sharp Edges
scabbards attached to the belt, and, because of the simplicity and usefulness, they were popular with the poorer classes. The wealthy carried them as well, usually finely made and ornate specimens. The English also carried quillon daggers, usually with no separate pommel, simply a butt. The blades might be curved or straight, single or double edged. There was always a definite ricasso, usually etched.

These were the popular knives in England during the 1600's, and they also came to the Americas with the English, although no specimens have been recovered, and no mention is made specifically to daggers. The Indians, however, noticed the knives and swords carried by the English colonists, and were fascinated by them. The called the newly arrived settlers, chauquaquock, or "knife-men". Knives were considered excellent trade items, as most Indians were willing to give most anything for one of the metal tools. Even the common table knife was a trade object, and the Indians sharpened them to use for skinning and dressing game.

Miles Standish, one of the pilgrims aboard the Mayflower, and one of the charter members of the Plymouth colony, once marched upon a party of Indians with eight men, and "caught the leaders alone, and knifed three to death in a fight. As a warning to others, Pilgrim soldiers returned displaying a bloody Indian head atop a pike." 12

Along with daggers, the plug bayonet came to America, to be used on the old rifles as a back up to save reloading in a pinch. These slipped into the rifle barrel, making it into an effective spear. It had it drawbacks, if too tight, it might not come out when the fighter had time to reload, and if too loose, might be left in the body of the enemy, or drop out before the fatal thrust, leaving the fighter completely helpless. These remained popular until the 1700's, when the socket bayonet, developed by a French engineer, Isaac de la Chaumette, in 1706, and improved upon by M. Deschamps in 1718, who developed a socket knife which could be fitted over the muzzle of a gun or inserted in to a handle for use as a belt knife. 13

As America was settled by many different nationalities, many different weapons were seen on her shores. The Scots, many who left Scotland after the rebellions in the 1730's and 40's, brought their own weapons, such as the Scottish dirk. This was similar to the kidney dagger, and usually had a wooden hilt deeply carved with interlacing

Vannoy

strapwork. Usually there was a plate of brass, pewter, or silver on the pommel. Many of these, especially those made after 1745, were fashioned from old swords. These were carried in sheaths, usually leather mounted in metal to match the pommel plates of the hilts. Some sheaths had a provision for an extra small knife or two or a knife and fork.

Folding knives were also popular in England, and many came to the American shores in the 17th century and are often found at archaeological sites. These were often one-bladed knives, with most being four, five or even up to seven inches long when closed, they were large knives.

One such knife was found, with one blade and a small cup for measuring powers, believed to have belonged to one of the first doctors in the new settlement.

Colonists also brought butcher knives, and common kitchen knives and table ware to the shores, and occasionally these blades, rusted and pitted, are found, a reminder of the tough men and women who forged a country out of the wilderness. These were the first white people to reach our shores, and they carried the first knives to the New World. The knife, it all forms, soon became a valuable tool, a fighting weapon, and a collectors item for the many different cultures that sprung up with the growing of the New World.

Sharp Edges

Castillo de San Marcos, an old Spanish Fort in St. Augustine, Florida. Construction completed in 1695.

Chapter 3
Knives of The Westward Expansion

After the colonies were well established, far seeing men looked to the West, and wondered what lay beyond the hills and valleys. Men like Daniel Boone, Davy Crockett, Lewis and Clark, and others set off into the unknown with little more than a few supplies, a gun, and a tomahawk and a knife. These were frontiersmen, the early prototype for the later mountain men, who explored the untamed mountains in search of furs.

In 1767, Boone, along with John Finley, John Stuart, and a few others, set off to the wilds of Kentucky, blazing a trail for others to follow. According to one description, Boone wore a fringed hunting shirt, deerskin leggings and moccasins. He carried a tomahawk and knife in his belt. They found the trail, a well used but narrow trail the Indians had used for generations, through the Cumberland Gap and into Kentucky.

One of the first references to a hunting knife carried by Daniel Boone was when he was courting his wife, Rebecca, where Boone proceeded to "try her temper." "Out of its sheath came the ever present hunting knife. Young Daniel, in apparent absentmindedness, began to cut idly at the green turf...Slash, slash, a pick and a cut at a blade of grass. The absent minded young man had cut a great hole in the precious garment. (A white cambric apron, priceless finery in the eyes of a frontier girl.)" [1]

Rebecca took the incident with good humor, and Boone married her on August 14, 1756.

Boone also used his knife to leave records of his travels, and carved in trees throughout Eastern Tennessee and North Carolina. One says, "D Boon killa bar on this tree, 1773." [2]

Sharp Edges

A blade, such as this blank, was used as a trade knife. Indians could attach their own custom handles (Author's Collection)

Vannoy

Although there has been controversy as to the authenticity of these various inscriptions, they are probably authentic, as one inscription of 1760 was know as early as 1770. Although expansion of the trees trunks stretched and distorted the lettering, it could not obliterated the deep carvings made by Boone's keen-edged hunting knife.

What kind of knife did Boone use on his travels? Most accounts say a hunting knife, and there were few manufactures around at that time making knives. One photograph of some of Boone's arms and traps shows a rather short butcher type knife, which was the standard hunting knife of the time. It has a rather full belly, and a spear point, with a slight guard between handle and blade. 3

Most were probably country made, or made by local blacksmiths for use as general purpose hunting knives. Possibly, the same makers that manufactured knives during the Revolutionary War, also made knives for the frontiersmen as well, although it is probably a good bet that most were local products, well made, and paid for, not in cash, but in barter, as was often the case among the frontier people, who had little ready cash to spare. Later exploration undoubtedly used more factory made products, such as Lewis and Clark, when they took many knives along with them for trade purposes.

When Jefferson bought the Louisiana Purchase from the French in 1803, he really had no idea if he purchased some land, or maybe a large expanse of ocean. In 1804, Jefferson sent his private secretary, Meriwether Lewis, and William Clark along with a party of explorers westward to explore the new lands.

Many of the knives taken on this expedition have been covered in a previous chapter, and it obvious by the trading they did that must have carried a great number of knives. But what of the knives that Lewis and Clark and their men used themselves on their travels? Knives were a necessity, for skinning and butchering game, and the other chores that only a knife could do.

Meriwether Lewis was known to have ordered a dagger on the order of a "Navy dirk" for use on the expedition, but was inadvertently left behind in Pittsburgh in July 1803. President Jefferson noticed the oversight, and notified Captain Lewis that he would forward the knife. Lewis replied that, "The dirk can not well come by post, nor is it of moment to me, the knives that were made at

Sharp Edges

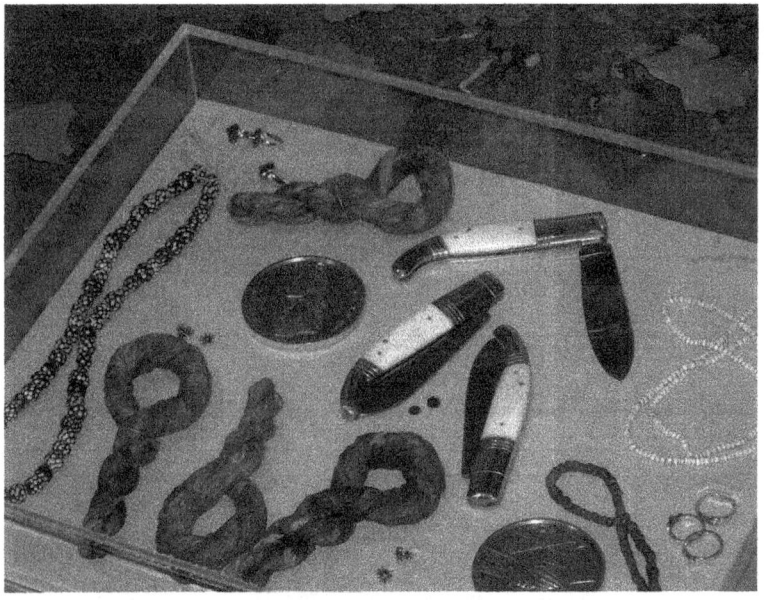

Several items used explorers opening up the west, including folding knives.
Photo by author taken in the Museum of the Westward Expansion, St. Louis Arch, St. Louis, MO.

Vannoy

Harper's Ferry will answer my purpose equally as well and perhaps better; it (the dirk) can therefore be taken care of until my return." According to Carl P. Russell, "The Harpers' Ferry knives mentioned by Lewis are presumed to be the ancestors of the U.S. rifleman's knife, the first model which appeared a quarter of a century after Lewis and Clark." No specimen of these 1803 knives has yet been found. 4

Fort Columbia, Washington has a clasp knife that was found in William Clark's properties in the Clark home in St. Louis. The single big blade is mounted under a metal bolster, with a spring extending part way down the back of the knife's handle. On the blade the letter "M" is stamped. Although there is no record that Clark carried this knife on the expedition, it is of the correct time frame to have been carried at that time.

In one instance, a knife saved a man's life in a very unusual way. The man's name was Windsor, and Lewis tells it in his journal. "who had sliped and fallen abut the center of this narrow pass and was lying prostrate on his belley, with his wright hand arm and leg over the precipice while he was holding on with the left arm and foot as well as he could which appeared to be with much difficulty. I discovered his danger and the trepidation which he was in gave me still further concern for I expected every instant to see him loose his strength and slip off; altho' much allarmed at his situation I disguised my feelings and spoke very calmly to him and assured him that he was in no kind of danger, to take the knife out of his belt behind him with his wright hand and dig a hole with it in the face of the bank to receive his wright foot which he did and then raised himself to his knees; I then directed him to take off his mockersons and to come forward on his hands and knees holding the knife in one hand and the gun in the other this he happily effected and escaped." 5

One journal entry mentions drying out metal goods that were wet after a September rainstorm. "I found on opening the goods that many of the articles were much injured; particularly the articles of iron, which wer rusted very much, my guns, tomehawks, & knives were of this class." After drying these items, he admitted them to baggs of oil-cloth. (Lewis, Sept. 17, 1803. 6

Another entry by Clark reads, "Friday 6th. (April, 1804) a Cloudy Day, river fall 10 Inches, the Bark Canoo set out for

Sharp Edges
Mackenaeck, give out Knives Tomahawkes &c.&c. to the men." 7

With the expanding of the United States boundaries came conflict, more often than not with the Indians, who had the land first, and were reluctant to give it up to the marauders. But the Indians weren't the only ones with prior claims. Since the 1500's, the Spanish had settled in California, Mexico, and the Southwest, and the Mexican government claimed the lands of Texas, New Mexico, and California for themselves. One of the most famous battles fought for land rights was between the Texans and the Mexicans at the Alamo near San Antonio, Texas. Davy Crockett, explorer from Tennessee, and Jim Bowie with his famous knife, both died there.

Crockett kept a journal of those days, and includes a description of Bowie's knife. "I found colonel Bowie, of Louisiana, in the fortress, a man celebrated for having been in more desperate personal conflicts than any other in the country, and whose name has been given to a knife of a peculiar construction, which is now in general use in the Southwest."

"While we were conversing, he had occasion to draw his famous knife to cut a strap, and I wish I may be shot if the bare sight of it wasn't enough to give a man of a squeamish stomach the cholic, especially before breakfast. He saw I was admiring it, and, said he, "Colonel, you might tickle a fellow's ribs a long time with this little instrument before you'd make him laugh; and many a time I have seen a man puke at the idea of the point touching the pit of stomach." 8

This was probably a true comment on the qualities of the Bowie knife.

Recently found in a public library in Bedford, Mass. is a knife that was given to Davy Crockett by Jim Bowie. In an article in the August, 1988 Blade magazine, Jim Taylor writes about seeing the Bowie knife, and why he, and other knife writers, accept that it is an authentic bowie knife. There is an old note that came with the knife, that says, "This is a Bowie knife-Given to Davy Crockett by Bowie-Davy Crockett gave it to Henry Clay-Henry Clay gave it to my father-My Grandfather Watkins and - Henry Clay - were half brothers. -Bowie and Crockett were both killed by-Mexicans in the Alamo, San Antonio; -Texas-Davy Crockett cut his name - in the case 1830 - Tom Watkins.

Although the evidence that the note is authentic is scanty,

Vannoy
several items ring true. Clay and Crockett knew each other well, and Clay had several half-brothers named Watkins, it is a very old note. The knife is very typical of early American made bowie knives, but there was no makers name to be found on the knife. The dimensions are: overall length, 15 1/2 inches long, with a 10 1/2 inch blade that is 1 3/4 inches wide. The handles are a solid piece of buffalo horn and the pommel, ferrule and crossguard are of nickel silver. It has a spear point with a false edge, ground only from one side. Crockett's name is indeed, scratched lightly but legibly into the nickel silver on the throat of the sheath. Even if the Crockett-Bowie link wasn't there, the knife is still an excellent example of an early American Bowie knife. 9

Of all the knives in the history of the U.S., none have had so many imitators as has the Bowie knife. Although Jim Bowie carried many knives at different times in his colorful life, the knife that was lost at the Alamo is the one that everyone speculates on. Because of this speculation, the Bowie knife has been kept in the spotlight. People research it, knife makers come up with their versions, and still everyone would like to find the original knife that Bowie carried at the Alamo.

Probably more has been written on the Bowie knife that any other knife in history, and were the original to be found, much of the writing would stop. The intriguing thing about the Bowie is that no one really knows just exactly what the knife looked like, or who really made it. Everyone speculates. Did it have a clip point, or a spear point? Bowies have been made both ways, with the clip point being the most widely accepted form. In 1916, Lucy Bowie, James sister, wrote: "In 1832, the brothers went North, Rezin wished to consult the celebrated Dr. Pepper, of Philadelphia, about his eyes. On that same northern trip he gave into the hands of a Philadelphia cutler the model of the Bowie knife. The cutler improved it and placed them on the market. The blade was shortened to eight inches; a curve was made in one side of the point and both edges were sometimes sharpened." According to William R. Williamson, in a article titled, "The American Bowie, Its Origin and Development, Knife Digest, April 10, 1974, the unnamed cutler was Henry Schively, who was listed in the directories in the late 1820's and early 1830's as "cutler and surgeons instrument mr. 75 Chestnut." Dr. Pepper lived at 225

Sharp Edges
Chestnut, not far from Shively's shop. Shively is credited for the clip point style of Bowie. 10
 Although a knife that was given to H.W. Fowler from Rezin Bowie himself has a modified spear point, rather than a clip point. That it was big is no doubt, but how big? One source says it was 11 inches long, 2 1/4 inches wide, and 3/8 inch thick. One observer, "P.Q." gave a clear description of the Bowie knife in 1838, "The blade measures twelve inches ...Observe it's edge - keen and smooth, and so perfect that a barber might use it in his trade. Its point is curved and hollowed at the back, cutting both ways, like a two-edged sword. It is two inches broad at the heel and of proportionate thickness. The weight, alone, is sufficient to give effect to a descending blow." 11.
Another account, attributed to Rezin Bowie, Jim's brother who designed the knife, it was 9 1/4 inches long and 1 1/2 inches wide. Rezin writes, in 1838, "The first Bowie knife was made by myself in the parish of Avoyelles, in this State, (Louisiana) as a hunting knife, for which purpose, exclusively, it was used for many years... Following are the fact respecting the manner in which Colonel James Bowie first became the possessor of this knife. He had been shot by an individual with whom he was at variance; and as I presumed that a second attempt would be made by the same person to take his life, I gave him the knife to be used as occasion might require, as a defensive weapon. Some time afterwards it was resorted to by Colonel James Bowie in a chance, rough fight between himself and certain other individuals with whom he was them inimical .... it was the means of saving his life. The improvement in its fabrication and the state of perfection which it has since acquired from experienced cutlers was not brought about through my agency." Jim used the knife in the famous Vidalia Sandbar fight, so it could claim the title of the "original Bowie". 12
 Bowie had been shot in the hip and stabbed with a sword cane, but killed Major Norris Wright, with the knife, and after being shot in the arm, wounded a second antagonist, Alfred Blanchard. In 1829 he used the knife again in a fight with a crooked gambler, John Sturdivant.
 In an article in the Jan/Feb 1978 American Blade Magazine, by William R. Williamson, he writes: "Rezin modeled the first Bowie

A belt knife, possibly a trade knife, complete with beaded sheath. Indians used white man's knives because it was easier than making their own out of rock. Photo by author, knife courtesy of Little Big Horn Battlefield National Moument, Crow Agency Montana.

Sharp Edges

after the Mediterranean dirk knife of "Spanish Dagger" as it was called in the South and Southwest of that period. This type was popular as a hunting knife and weapon before and after the introduction of the Bowie knife." 13

According to William R. Williamson, a blacksmith on the Bowie plantation, Jesse Cliffe, did the actual work of making the knife under Rezin's supervision. Rezin also gave a number of presentation knives to various friends, including Governor E.D. White of Louisiana; Lieutenant H.W. Fowler, U.S. Dragoons; Edwin Forrest, the famous 19th century actor; and others.

Rezin had a personal knife made for him by Henry Schively of Philadelphia, PA, that was the forerunner of the Bowie. It is a butcher-type knife, with a heavy blade, coin silver mounts and a handsome silver sheath. Rezin later gave this knife to Jesse Perkins of Natchez, Mississippi.

Some say the Bowie knife was Jim's invention, some say Rezin's, and others feel a blacksmith named James Black modified Bowie's design and he made the knife. However, one foremost Bowie Knife expert puts little credence to the Black story, and writes, "There is no evidence to support the legend. On the contrary, there is fact to discredit it." Ben Palmer, "The Legend of James Black." 14

Although in Bowie-Knife by Raymond Thorp says, "James Black, before his blindness, made hundreds of Knives "like Bowie's" in design and temper of steel." 15 To date, not a single knife has been found that has a mark that could be James Blacks. Not a single authentic James Black knife has ever been discovered. Unless further evidence turns up, we can probably lay the James Black legend to rest, and attribute the knife to Rezin. But however it came about, the knife worked it way into American legends.

Bowie and his new knife opened the way for the bowie knife era. In one fight he killed three ruffians that Sturdivant had hired to kill him. He supposedly cut off the head of one, disemboweled the second, and caught the third as he tried to run, splitting his head in two, all with the huge bowie knife.

After Bowie's exploits with the knife, other frontiersmen wanted "a knife like Bowie's" and many cutlers, including those in Sheffield, brought out knives with several variations, all classed as "Bowie knives. American makers who marketed Bowie knives

Vannoy

included Shively in Philadelphia; Searles in Baton Rouge; Alfred Hunter, of Newark, NJ; Samuel Bell, of Knoxville, TN; Chevalier, of New York; Marks & Rees of Cincinnati, to name but a few.

In 1838, an Arkansas traveler, William Bailey wrote of his adventures through Southern North America. Staying in one of the inns along his travels, he found it necessary to share a room with two state senators, who, ".... fairly bristled with weapons; each had two enormous "Bowie-knives" in his belt which were at least fifteen inches in length, and a brace of pistols." 16

Although the maker is unknown, one of "Bowie's Knives" was given to a man in New Orleans by one "Juan Padillo, who left the LaFitte band of pirates to follow the fortunes of Bowie."

The knife is of tempered steel, the blade sixteen inches long, with a steel guard and a buckhorn handle. The handle is dressed smooth where the hand clasps it, and on one side is a silver plate one and one-half inches long, set into the handle, on which is scratched, in rude characters, Jim Bowie. On the steel guard of the knife, on the upper side, two notches have been cut with a file, which old Juan Padillo said were cut to mark the number of men Bowie had killed with the weapon. On the lower side of the guard are three notches, which are said to represent the number of Indians scalped with the knife. The knife was given by Bowie to Padillo while the former was a resident of San Augustine, Texas; and was presented by Padillo to its present owner in 1862, when the latter succeeded in recovering from the Comanches ten head of horses, which they had stolen from Padillo's ranch thirty-five miles west of San Antonio. The most famous battle that Bowie and his knife were in was at the Alamo, where, sick with fever, "Bowie was waiting when the enemy rushed into the dark chapel. Pistols flamed from his cot. For seconds the famous Bowie knife slashed right and left before sabers and bayonets thrust past it and it fell from a dead hand." 17

From there on, no one knows what happened to the famous knife, but through the years following the Alamo up to the Civil War, nearly every factory made it's own style of Bowie knife, and men wanting to look like the West bought them. The West gave the Bowie knife a whole new realm to conquer. Both before and after the Civil War, men went west, looking for adventure, land, gold, or to see what was over the next hill.

Sharp Edges

A replica of a Bowie knife with a spear point and a guard on the handle.. (Author's collection)

Chapter 4
Knives of the Revolutionary War

After the colonies became self-supporting, and began to chaff under the restrictions and taxation levied by the king across the sea, it was decided to make the blow for independence, to become a nation in their own right, rather than "colonies" of some distance, unconcerned country.

The American Revolution was fought by men who had only one thing going for them, the dream of freedom. They had little money; many were never paid for their services. They had little or no military training, and weapons that were not the best. "Squirrel guns," that is, smooth-bore muskets, captured British weapons, and the famous Kentucky rifle, all played a part in the War for Independence. Knives, swords, and bayonets also played an important role in the War.

According to American Knives, by Harold Peterson, many of the men who fought in the American army, had long since given up the large sheath knife in favor the smaller jackknife. In fact, some states required soldiers to carry a pocketknife of some sort. Many of the "frontiersmen" who joined up still carried the large sheath knife, often a kitchen butcher knife fitted with a belt sheath, or simply stuck into the belt.

In the book, Red Dawn at Lexington, Louis Birnbaum, Houghton Mifflin, 1986, writes of the beginning of the war. "Each member of the regiment, if he did not own an effective firearm, was equipped with one by the committee - either musket or a rifle - a bayonet if obtainable, pouch, knapsack, and thirty cartridges."

"There were no distinctive uniforms among the colonial troops until late in the Revolutionary War. The blue and buff usually associated with American Revolutionary soldiers were the Virginia

Sharp Edges

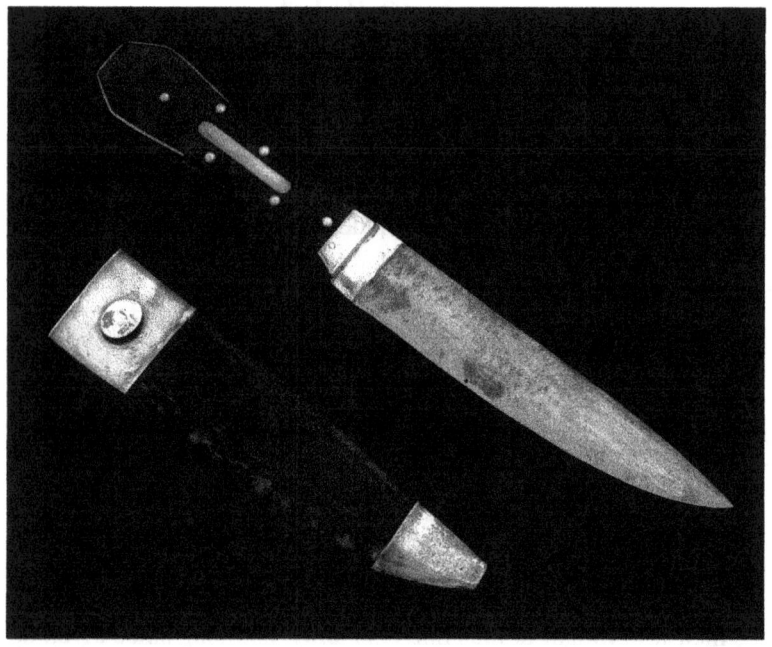

Carrigan guardless bowie type knife made by James Black, Arkansas, c. 1830. From the collection of the Historic Arkansas Museum, Little Rock, Arkansas. Gift of Mary Delia Carrigan Prather.

Vannoy

militia colors and would not make their appearance until the arrival of George Washington as commander-in-chief in July 1775 ...and if any distinctive uniform could be said to be common among the men, it was the frontiersman's shirt, soon to become famous as the rifle shirt."

"The shirt hung to just below the knees and was worn cinched at the waist with a large leather belt from which usually hung a tomahawk and knife." This shirt became associated, in the minds of the British, with the deadly marksmanship of the frontier. For that reason Washington recommended in 1776 that his entire army wear the shirt. "It is the dress which is justly supposed to carry no small terror to the enemy, who think every such person is a complete marksman." 1

Although many soldiers carried knives of some type, a special group of soldiers developed a specialized style of knife. These soldiers were the riflemen, who carried mainly the newer "rifled" barreled guns, which owed its origin to the German Jaeger, a heavy hunting weapon with a rifled barrel.

The Pennsylvania Dutch improved on the gun, making the bore smaller, the barrel longer and lighter, and the replacing the heavy stock with a lighter one. Although perfected by the Pennsylvanians, the Kentucky riflemen used the rifle enough and made it famous under the name, Kentucky Rifle. Unlike the earlier rifles, these rifles relied for their accuracy on a ball that fitted the bore tightly and thus would take the spin impacted by the rifle grooves. The fit was achieved by wrapping the ball in a greased patch of cloth before it was rammed down the barrel.

In American Knives, Peterson writes: "Sometimes a rifleman had his patches cut in advance, but at other times he had to trim them as he loaded his gun. Then he needed a knife. The big "scalping" knife in his belt could be used for this purpose, but often he carried a smaller, handier knife in or attached to his rifle bag. These rifle knives were made in a great variety of patterns. Usually the blade was three or four inches long, and the handle might be wood, antler, or even cow horn. The early ones were unusually crude and unattractive. In the nineteenth century some handsome rifle knives with inlaid hilts were made by gunsmiths to match the decoration of the rifle." 2

Sharp Edges

A modern reproduction of a patch knife, similar to those used by the soldiers in the Revolutionary War. (Author's Collection)

Vannoy

While the rifleman's scalping knife, and the private's jackknife were mentioned in the regulations, some soldiers, particularly officers, carried daggers. These were of many different makes, and many different styles, having only the double-edged blade, the small size, around 6 inches, and usually guards in the form of a cross quillons. They ranged from hand forged, to highly ornate knives with silver mountings. These were unofficial, and not regarded as a fighting or survival weapon, although as a last resort, they could serve as a defense.

By far the most common edged weapons were swords and bayonets. Many references are made to both in the writings of the period as well as newer works. Most officers carried swords, there were dress swords, and foot officer swords, and cavalry swords. Bayonets were fixed to the rifle barrel, and saw use in both the continental army and the British troops. Due to the shortage of weapons among the colonies, many men also carried improvised spears.

Sketches and paintings of the era tell more than do diaries and journals. Many soldiers are immortalized by the artists' hand, and many of these paintings and simple sketches show the soldier with a knife at his side, such as a drawing of one of Morgan's riflemen, who is shown with a large knife in plain view on his belt.

In the book, Collectors Illustrated History of the Revolutionary War, George C. Neumann and Frank J. Kravic, Stackpole, 1975, it pictures and describes some common knives used during the war. "The knife is usually defined as having a single edged blade - thus qualifying for a variety of uses ranging from fighting to daily chores. It was necessity on the frontier and also accompanied most regular soldiers as a belt or pocketknife." 3

There were a wide variety of knife styles common to the era, and a wide variety of styles evacuated from campsites of the war. They ranged from ordinary butcher style knives, similar in design to the later Dadley and Green River knives, through a Hudson Highland short knife, about 11 inches overall, a dagger made from a cut down silver mounted hunting sword, a knife fashioned from an old scythe blade, 9 1/4 inches long, and the "riflemen patch knives" which looked like a stub bladed paring knife. One shown has an antler handle. 4

Sharp Edges

Also found were large pocketknives, usually with one blade and often with horn handles. There was a variety of smaller, one bladed pocketknife, and the knife and fork combination sets for camp usage, and an early Barlow knife, circa 1780-1820.

Several folding knives have been at various forts and campsites used during the revolution. New York and New Hampshire required their militia to carry pocketknives. Some makers marketed folding knife and fork sets, which folded into a pocket-knife like handle and were easier to carry and less likely to be lost than individual table ware.

Two folding knives now reside in the Alexandria-Washington Lodge No. 22 that are credited to George Washington. One is a penknife with a clipped point and an offset blade, and another one is a late 18th century pocket-pruning knife, with a horn handle.

Thomas Jefferson carried a penknife with a blunt, spey-type blade, and tradition states that he used it to clean the mud from his boots.

Daggers also found a following among those rich enough to afford the extravagance. Daggers were developed as a fighting tool, usually two edged and spear pointed. Although unofficial weapons, many were carried as personal arms - especially by the frontiersmen and militia who often lacked bayonets for close infighting. These ranged from fancy European made daggers, such as one with an ivory handle, to one made from an old file and fitted with an antler handle.

Harold L. Peterson gives us a good description of the riflemen knives used during the time of the Revolutionary war. "The American Frontiersman lived daily in the shadow of attack from Indian warriors of wild beasts. He needed a good knife to protect himself in hand-to-hand combat once his rifle had been fired. He also needed a knife for general work in the woods. To meet these requirements a single knife had to be sturdy and large enough to serve as a weapon, yet not so big that it was unwieldy for camp duties. Because the frontiersman had few manufacturing facilities and little money to expend on ornamentation, his knife was usually simple, the blade forged by a local blacksmith or ground out of an old file and the haft a simple piece of wood or antler." 5

It is difficult if not impossible to say for sure that a given

Vannoy

knife was used during the Revolutionary war. According to Peterson, only one knife can actually be documented as having been a knife of the era, as specimens differ little from the 1700's to the 1800's. Written evidence is practically non-existent, and often what there is refers to the knives as "scalpers" or "butcher knives".

It is safe to assume, from samples found and written evidence, that daggers and butcher knives were used. Daggers were mainly fighting tools, and butcher knives all-purpose camp and fighting knives. Daggers were usually carried in a scabbard of harness leather or rawhide, sewn to fit the knife. Many daggers were worn as decoration. Perhaps by an officer attending a ball, who didn't want to carry a long sword. Many were mounted in silver and complete with silver scabbards, and dates range from the 1790's through the 1830's. Fancy presentation daggers were made as late as 1860. Butcher knives were more often than not worn thrust through the belt, usually carried far enough to the front so as not to interfere with the powder horn and hunting bag hung under the arm.

The hunting bag was similar to the later bag of "possibles" carried by the mountain men. Made of leather, this was carried slung over the shoulder, riding on the hip. Often, the powder horn was attached to the hunting bag, and one example has a scabbard for the patch knife sewn on so it is easily reached. According to the Illustrated History, a hunting bag might contain, "a steel striker, flints, cloth patches, a Jew's harp, tow (for cleaning, wadding and tinder), a leather bullet bag, a piece of trade lead, ladle, bullet mold, priming powder horn, a small animal butchering hatchet (9 1/2 inches long), a folding knife, an oval tobacco container, and a clay pipe." 6

After Cornwallis surrendered at Yorktown, the Continental Army pretty well disbanded. On June 2, 1784, Congress discharged the 700 members of the Continental line, leaving only eighty to guard military stores at West Point and Fort Pitt. The very next day, they asked for 700 men to serve for one year to protect the Western Frontier from the danger of Indian attack.

Then, due to strangulation of American trade, and the impressment of Yankee seamen into the Royal Navy, and other problems with England, the U.S. declared war on Great Britain on June 18, 1812. The call went out for more men.

Sharp Edges

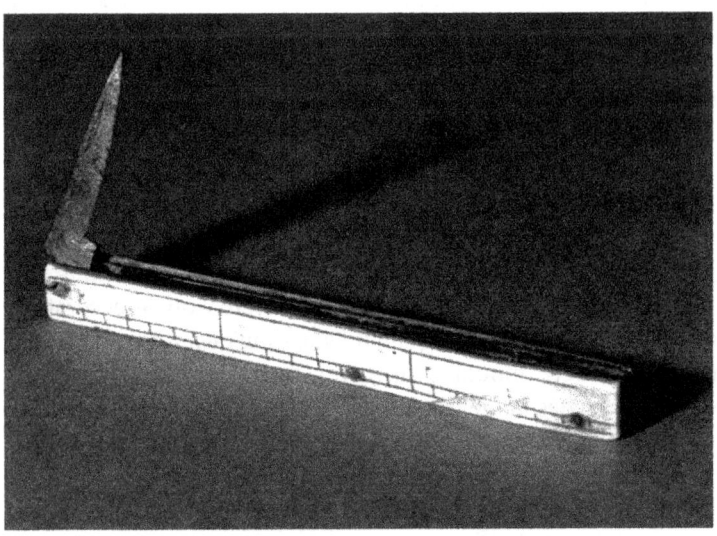

Measuring knife of steel with ivory. L 10.6, H .6, blade L 2.9 cm
Guilford Courthouse National Military Park, GUCO 92

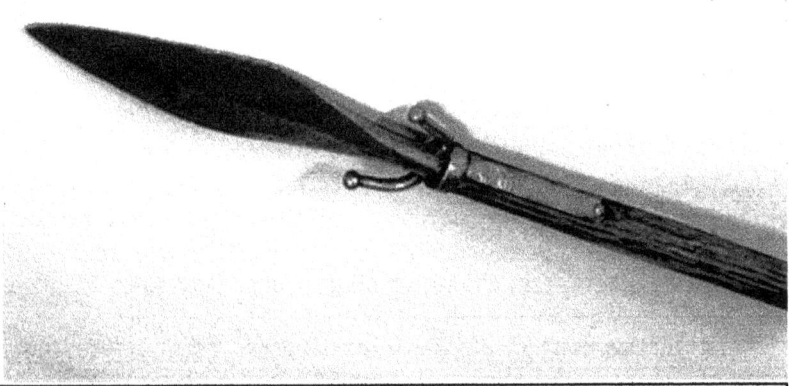

Spontoon head with piece of modern pole inserted. Said to have been carried at the Battle of Alamance, May 16, 1771, as well as the Battle of Guilford Courthouse.
Iron. L 31.8, W 5.1 cm Blade L 21.8, W 5.1 cm
Guilford Courthouse National Military Park, GUCO 27

Vannoy
action. In the book, and The U.S. Cavalry, an Illustrated History, Gregory J.W. Urwin, describes a typical Kentucky privates dress: ".... The arms, a rifle or musket, a tomahawk and butcher knife - those who do not furnish their own arms will be furnished." 7

This unit, under Colonel Richard M. Johnson, saw action in October of 1813, when they came upon 830 British soldiers and several of Chief Tecumseh's braves near River Thames, some eighty-five miles east of Detroit. Johnson's 500 mounted men charged. "The Redcoats got off two volleys and possibly a third, then the Kentuckians came ripping through them, shooting men at point-blank range, and maiming others with knives and tomahawks." 9. After this decisive victory, the Indians gave little trouble.

Although the new United States had no navy per say, in 1775 the Continental Congress became convinced of a need for a navy, and created a Marine Committee of the Congress to see to it. This committee remained in force during the war.

This committee organized several merchant ships as well as thirteen quality frigates, ranging in size from 14 to 32 guns. Crews were made up of men from all walks of life, often criminals, or men who were down-on-their-luck frequented the wrong saloon one night and awoke the next day with a headache aboard a ship bound for God knows where. The navy also enlisted a few pirates, giving them license as "privateers" or independent merchant ships. Merchant ships, likewise, carried licenses allowing them to carry arms and capture merchantmen of the other side. One thing the licenses did, if the ship was captured, the crews were treated as prisoners of war, not as criminals.

Sailors such as John Paul Jones, Nicolas Biddle, John Barry, and later during the War of 1812, Stephan Decatur and William Bainbridge, did their part with the early, sometimes barely seaworthy ships, to harass and engage the English fleets.

The navy developed it's own type of knives; most sailors carried jackknives to cut the ropes and do other chores that required a knife. One such knife has been found in the wreckage of a revolutionary war era English ship, off the coast of Yorktown. In an article in the National Geographic Magazine, there is a photograph of the brass handles; the steel blade has long since rusted away. The knife is Sheffield made.

Sharp Edges

Many officers and midshipmen carried dirks, as a companion to and substitute for the sword, and it combined the most fascinating characteristics of each. Considered a part of an officer's uniform, the dirks were often decorated handsomely. Yet it was a short, very effective weapon as well as an adornment. There are very few references to dirks or daggers in writings of the period, yet it is assumed that they have been worn since the first American set foot on a ship, but no record exists before 1802, when it was mentioned in naval regulations that dirks not be worn on shore. Later, in 1813, the navy again addressed the subject, saying that officers must wear swords with full dress uniforms, but may carry dirks with their undress uniforms.

Several dirks resemble small swords, with decorated grips, often of bone or ivory, often covered with mother-of-pearl. Many made after 1800 had curved blades, rather than the straight, dagger-like blade. Most of the navel dirks had blades around 10 inches, with anything from 9" up to 16" being common. Although there is little record of American suppliers making dirks during the Revolutionary War, in the book, Naval Officers Sword, London, several styles are on display in the National Maritime Museum, Greenwich, and undoubtedly the same style of dirk was used in America, many by English makers. Most of the dirks mentioned in the book were carried by English midshipmen, and ranged from an 8" blade to a 16 1/4 inch blade. Many were very ornate, such as one presentation dirk, which was "Damascened in blue and gold" with the hilt being a "lion's head pommel and back-piece, mane extending only one-third down the back, white ivory grip lower part diamond knurled; the gilt (double) chain for knuckle guard is missing." The hilt is 4 3/8 inches overall. The date given was 1824.

Most dirks, however, were not fancy, like the midshipman dirk believed to have been made between 1795 and 1805, although the hilt is "gilt octagonal pommel, fluted white ivory grip with gilt band round the centre...." The blade is, "straight, flat back, one groove up to the point, which is a double-edged spear point. Length, 14 3/4 inches, width 7/8 inch. Plain steel, no engraving."

Although the above-described dirks are English, there is reason to believe that American dirks were much the same pattern, and possibly, were even made by the same makers in England.

Vannoy

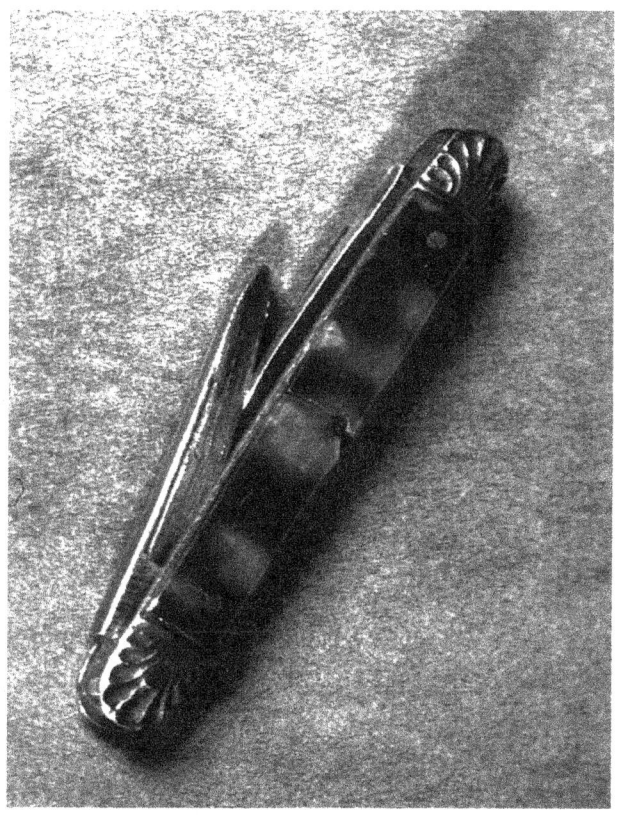

Pen knife, with Steel and tortoise shell. H .5, W 1.0, L 6.0 cm Guilford Courthouse National Military Park, GUCO 1560

Sharp Edges

The new navy saw some action during the Revolutionary War, but saw even more during the war of 1812, where officers such as Stephan Decatur, Captain Samuel Chester Reid, Captain William Bainbridge, commander of the Constitution, later nicknamed, Old Ironsides, made names for themselves. Decatur was one of the more romantic figures in the war, and a brilliant navel commander. One famous battle concerns a ship, the Philadelphia, which had been successful in blockading the harbor of Tripoli in the fall of 1803, and had ran upon a reef. The ship was captured, and Commodore Preble send Decatur capture the ship, destroy it if necessary to keep the Tripolitans from using it against the Americans. Decatur and his crew found the Philadelphia, and, with great stealth, sailed their ship close enough to board her. "The weapons were cold steel, the watchword, "Philadelphia". No firearms were used, for Preble's orders had been to "carry all with the sword."

"Without cheers and with desperate energy the little band dashed at the masses of astonished and terrified men before them, and the whistle of the cutlasses, the ring of steel against steel, the thud of the pike as it buried itself in some beating heart, alone gave evidence of the fell purpose of the stern boarders." 10 They captured the ship, and torched it.

Although not mentioned in the various writings of battles, Decatur carried a small dirk, which is now in the U.S. Naval Academy Museum.

Captain Samuel Reid, son of an English navel officer, but fighting for the American's, commanded a ship called the General Armstrong. Reid one day encountered an English ship, the Carnation, that drew them into battle. After heavy fighting, the British tried to board the American ship, only to be beaten back. "The cheers, shouts, curses and groans of the desperate men, mad with the blood lust of the fight, the ringing of steel on steel, as sword gritted against sword, or ax crashed on boarding cap, or bayonet crossed half-pike in the dreadful fray..." 11

Cold steel: Swords, bayonets, knives, boarding pikes, played their part aboard the ships on both sides of the conflict. Hand to hand fighting was often encountered as sailors tried to board the ships, and either succeeded or were beaten back.

The revolutionary army, undermanned, with inferior

Vannoy

weapons, took on what was, at the time, the world's most powerful empire, Great Britain, not once but twice, and won. This was a remarkable achievement in 1820, the U.S. had 9,638,453 people listed on the census, and in 1821 Great Britain had 15,472,000 people, not quite twice the population of the new country. As the author's father wisely put it, "Good thing there was so much ocean separating us from England." That, coupled with the guerrilla warfare tactics practiced by the colonist, caused England to surrender.

An unquenchable will to be free, and a strong fighting spirit, led the American troops to victory in 1781, and, although not mentioned overmuch in the writings of the period, but often shown in old prints made by trained and semi-skilled artists, the knife was right there alongside the fighting men, a necessary tool, and a deadly weapon when needed.

Sharp Edges

Chapter 5
Knives of the Mountain Men

The first explorers to reach the Western half of the United States, after Lewis and Clark determined that there was actually land out there, were the mountain men, trappers, looking for fortunes in "soft gold" or beaver and other furs. Beaver hats were the rage in Europe, and among the high and hope-to-be high society in American cities. With the demand for beaver, there was money to be made west of the Mississippi, where, it was said, the land was full of all kinds of animals just for the taking.

Fur had been a steady business in Canada since Samuel de Champlain saw the rich furs the Iroquois took along the St. Lawrence in 1610. By 1611, many of the earlier trapping regions of the St. Lawrence were practically depleted, and competition was fierce, with the English, French and Dutch competing for a slice of the fur market.

In Canada, much of the fur trapping was done by Indians or 'breeds, who knew the country, and the animals they trapped. In exchange for hides, the Indians were given white men's goods, cloth, steel knives, axes, and other goods. This flourishing trade continued for nearly 200 years, started by the French and carried on by the Hudson Bay Company, started in 1670.

Business in Canada flourished for the Hudson Bay Company. The first expedition send to North America by the Hudson Bay Company carried 200 fowling pieces, 400 powder horns, shot, 200 brass kettles, twelve gross of French knives, two gross of amber beads, and about 500 to 600 hatches. One good beaver pelt would bring the trapper either a half-pound of powder, four pounds of shot, one hatchet, eight jackknives, half a pound of beads, a good coat, or a pound of tobacco. 1

While the fur trade in Canada relied heavily on the Indian trappers, the fur trade in the U.S. created it's own hero's. Between the

Vannoy

years 1824-1838, rugged, adventurous "mountain men" explored the mountains and valleys of the west, looking for money and adventure. Of the former, there was little, of the latter, much. Wild animals, wilder Indians, severe weather conditions, and other dangers lurked in the new country. The men who took to this life fell into many classes, some were ruffians, looking for a place where they were not leashed by society, some were young, and many were learned men, who kept diaries and journals, or wrote books about the rugged life.

One such learned man was James Clyman, who accompanied William H. Ashley and Andrew Henry west in 1823. Clyman was described as wearing the "only original American costume.... the fringed buckskin suit," with powder horn, shot pouch, tomahawk, knife, maybe a pistol and certainly a muzzle loader, the mountain man was self-supporting, independent, and downright dangerous." 2
This became the costume of the mountain men, and of the essential weapons, perhaps none was more essential than his knife.

Probably more than any other place in the annuals of American's history, has a knife played as important a part in the lives of men as it did during the fur trapping years.

Not only was the knife a tool for skinning beaver, and properly fleshing the hide, it was also an integral part of the mountain man's equipment. Knives were used for skinning and cleaning game for the cook pot, for cutting small branches for bedding and making stretchers for beaver pelts and as weapons. If he carried a muzzle-loading rifle, he might also carry a small patch knife, as was used by the riflemen in the Revolutionary War.

A mountain man was seldom far from his knife. Bernard DeVoto, in his epic on the fur trade, Across the Wide Missouri, gives us a look at the mountain man's way of life.
As evening fell, the trappers would find a likely spot for and evening meal and a rest for the night. Fires were lit, and buffalo, or other wild game, was roasted over the fires. When the meal was cooked, the smell of roasting meat mingling with the smell of pine and wood smoke, the mountain men, "sitting cross legged on the ground, using only their Green River knives, would eat their way through six or ten pounds of fat (buffalo) cow." 3

Sharp Edges

A Green River Knife and a buffalo skull. (Author's Collection)

Vannoy

As the evening lengthened into night, the storytelling session, which consisted of who could tell the tallest yarn, had spun on, "Till at last the fire sank. The mountain men rolled up in his robe or blanket... loaded rifle beside him, and knife and pistols within reach, and might lie awhile listening to the wind and the water and the coyotes." 4

Usually a mountain man carried more than one knife. A large "camp knife" was carried in the pack on a horse or mule, and used for the heavy chores around camp such as hacking meat off a buffalo carcass, cutting branches for a bed, and other such chores. These knives were large, around twelve inches or so, with 8" or longer blades. Several of these camp type knives were imported into the U.S. from the factories at Sheffield, England. One such knife is a representative of the period. It bears the marks, "Jukes Coulson, Stokes & Co." a Sheffield firm. It has a horn handle, held to the hilt by oversized rivets holding brass washers and by a heavy ferrule riveted to the front end of the hilt. The blade is about 8 1/2 inches long, and fairly thick. Many knives of this type were imported into Canada for use by the Hudson Bay Company trappers, and were dubbed, "Hudson Bay Knives." Unwin and Rodgers, another Sheffield firm, manufactured and imported knives of this type, bearing the mark, "V (crown) R/ Unwin & Rodgers/Cutlers, Sheffield;" and in a scroll is the marking, "SUPERLATIVE". Knives such as these, bearing the VR mark, were manufactured after 1837. 5

Two other distinct knives were put to use by the mountain men. One was a skinner, and one was a butcher, or bowie knife. Although practically any knife will work for skinning game, and a mountain man wasn't real picky about what he used, as long as it did the job, and the mountain man was good at improvising when it didn't. When a mountain man needed a skinning knife, he often reground a knife to put the bevel on one edge to avoid slashing the hide. If he had no knife, often, he made one.

Several knives have been found that were fashioned from old files, saw blades, and the like. Jim Baker, who trapped and scouted throughout the Rockies for many years, owned two handmade knives, one made from a file, and one with a "country-made" blade. Another country made blade, heavy enough for the chopping block but also small enough to be put to work as a scalper or general purpose knife,

Sharp Edges

was found in Jackson Hole, Wyoming, in 1924, at the site of a trappers camp. Fitted with wood or stag handles, these knives were serviceable for many years in the wild.

As the knife was such a common place implement to the trapper, in his writings he seldom referred to it as anything other than a "knife," "butcher knife," "bowie knife," or "Green River Knife." Most references were simply to knives, skinning knives or bowie knives. If a mountain man carried a muzzleloader, he might also carry a small "patch knife" for cutting patches for his gun, like those carried by the riflemen in the Revolution. The manufactures and makers of knives were not often referred to. Where a man might say he carried a "Hawken" rifle, he would usually refer to a knife as simply his knife.

Seeing they were missing out, it didn't take the manufactures long to note that a new market for a specialized type of knife was springing up on the slopes of the Rockies. A skinning knife, with the blade curved in an upward sweep, with the bevel on one side only to avoid slashing the hide. A fairly rounded, rather than a pointed, tip.

Company ledgers can tell some of the story, as do the knives themselves, when the marks have not been rusted or ground away. A large percentage of knives came west from Sheffield prior to about 1836, when J. Russell in Massachusetts, began putting out knives.

One knife that is referred to by name, and that still sparks a controversy among knife collectors, is the Green River Knife, or the phrase, "Give it to them up Green River." Many historians, such as Bernard DeVoto, feel this refers to knives shipped prior to 1837, that bore the mark, G (Crown) R, meaning Georgius Rex, or King George, the ruler of England before Victoria. One such knife, found on Camp Creek in Jackson Hole, Wyoming, bears the mark, G (Crown) R, with the word, Furnis underneath. This referred to the Furness brothers of Stannington, who brought their knives to Sheffield to be shipped abroad for trade.

To the mountain men, many who cared less about who sat on the English throne, G.R. meant the Green River, or the Green, in Wyoming, where many rendezvous were held. In fact, some of these knives were probably in the shipment of goods that William H. Ashley sold at his first Green River Rendezvous in 1825, perhaps contributing to the name "Green River" for the knives.

Resting against a buffalo skull is a butcher-type knife blade, the type that was traded during the Mountain Man era. These blades were shipped west, and handles of either wood, bone or antler were added by the new owners. (Author's Collection)

Sharp Edges

Although the knives bearing the G.R. were the first knives to reach fur country, American makers were not far behind. J.Russell & Co, Green River Massachusetts, began manufacturing knives around 1836. These knives, the Green River Knife, and the Green River Dadley, where often found in the mountain man's regalia. The Green River Knife, or Green River Skinner, was about eight or nine inches long, with an upswept blade, beveled on one side, strictly for skinning. The Dadley was a straight bladed butcher type knife, with a spear point, used for utility chores around camp, and butchering buffalo or other game for the stew pot. Russell's knives bear the stamp, J. R. Russell & Co., Green River Works, on the blade, and it was later imitated by I. Wilson Cutlers in Sheffield, and their knives bear the mark, Green River, a cloverleaf and a diamond, I Wilson, Sycmore St., Sheffield, England, with the notation, "Hand Forged" near the hilt. Many of these came into fur country as well. Without knowing when the mountain men coined the phrase, "Give it to them up to Green River," it is difficult to know which knife was being referred to. It could have been either or both knives.

Knives were acquired each year by trappers at the annual rendezvous, where the trappers and merchants got together to buy, sell, trade, drink whiskey, spin tales, dance with the Indian women or each other, and collect the necessary supplies for another year in the wilderness. From 1824 - 1840, except for the year 1831, these gala parties were held in the middle of the trappers country, many around the Jackson Hole area of Wyoming, and surrounding areas.

These were a money making venture for the traders, and they usually came out ahead of the trappers. There were two classes of trappers working the Rockies for furs, the "free trapper," who trapped on his own or with a small group, and sold his furs to the highest bidders, and the "skin trappers," who signed on with a company, and the company paid for the outfit and the trapper agreed to sell his furs to the company that staked him. Having some bargaining power made the free trappers come out a little ahead of the skin trappers, but they still have to pay the tremendous mark-up on goods for the next season's supplies.

In Firearms, Traps and Tools, Carl Russell gives us a look at knife prices at the 1825 Green River, Wyo. Rendezvous, initiated by William H. Ashley. "Twenty free trappers at this meeting bought

Vannoy

knives of several different kinds and grades, paying from $.40 to $2.75 apiece. The ordinary butcher knives sold to the trappers brought $1.50 to $2.00 each." 6 In 1827, Ashley committed in writing to bring merchandise from St. Louis to Bear Lake, Idaho, and sell goods to the firm of Smith, Jackson, and Sublette at specified wholesale prices. The price for a butcher knife was $.75." 7

In 1832, free trapper Johnson Gardner purchased several knives from $2.00 each at the Fort Union American Fur Company Post. In 1835, the AFC purchased similar knives in St. Louis for $.15 to $.18 each.

In 1833, the Rocky Mountain Fur Company listed, among other commodities, 100 dozen 'common scalper', and 35 dozen more expensive knives for "murder with style." 8 The common scalpers sold to trappers for $1.50 to $2.00 each. The RMFC paid about $.20 each for them, a 100% mark up. 1833 was also the high year for beaver, with a good pelt, or plew, bringing around $6.00. A man had to trap a lot of beaver.

Knives might be home made, or bargained for at the rendezvous, but however they were obtained, they were a necessity in the rough, wild country the mountain man traveled in. Although most often used as tools, knives were also called upon as defense weapons against hostile Indians, whites, or wild animals. Although most mountain men, if given the choice, preferred to use a muzzleloader or pistol for self-defense, often they had little choice in the matter.

Grizzly bears were common to the country, and, although encounters between mountain men and grizzlies were few, they did happen. Jedediah Smith, one educated mountain man who kept extensive journals of his life, and was religious, clean-shaven, and abstained from tobacco and liquor, except an occasional glass of wine, had one encounter that ended with him losing an ear from the attack. As James Clyman wrote in his journals about the attack, Smith didn't have time to reach for his belt knife before the bear, "catching (Smith) by the ball pouch and butcher knife which he broke but breaking several ribs and cutting his head badly." 9 Andrew Sublette, one of the Sublette brothers, decided to test the mettle of a grizzly. He wounded the bear with his muzzleloader, then, with only his bear dog and an unloaded gun, fought off not only the wounded

Sharp Edges

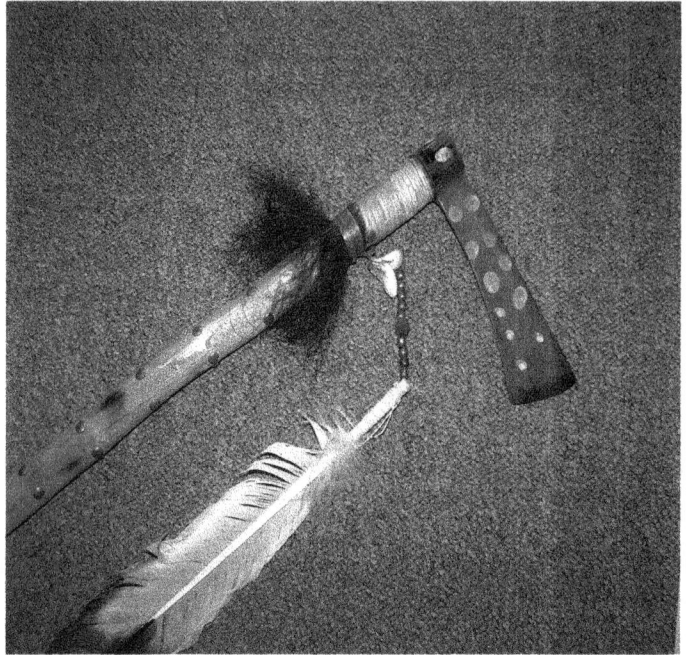

Although a little more ornate than would be used on the frontier, as this one was made for the tourist trade, a traditional tomahawk was used by both Indians and trappers for defense and utility. Author's collection.

Vannoy

grizzly but also its mate as well using only his belt knife. He survived, but was badly wounded and never fully recovered.

Probably the most famous account of a bear attack was the story of Hugh Glass, who not only fought the grizzly bear, but, after being left for dead by his companions, fought his way nearly two hundred miles to a fort to find help. In the novel, Lord Grizzly, Frederick Mansfred describes the fight.

"He hugged her(the bear). And hugging her, at last got his knife around and set. He punched. His knife punged through the tough hide and slipped into her belly just below the ribs with and easy slishing motion. He stabbed again. Again and again. The knife punged through the tough furred hide each time then slid in easy." 10

Occasionally knives were used as defense against Indians or other whites. In Jed Smith's journals, he describes a fight between his party and a party of Mohave Indians. Several men were killed, and the party was armed with only five guns and their butcher knives. Smith wrote; "with our knives we lopped down small trees in such a manner as to clear a place to stand. The fallen poles formed a slight breastwork, and to ends of some of the lighter poles we fastened our butcher knives with cords so as to form a tolerable lance." 11

Fiction brought in knife play more than did the factual accounts of the period. In two fiction based on real life novels by ex-mountain men, they mention the "Green River Knives."

In Life in the Far West, Frederick Ruxton gives a lively description of a fight between trappers and Mexicans. "...(The Mexicans) gave way and bolted through the door, leaving the floor strewed with wounded, many most dangerously; for, as may be imagined, a thrust from the keen scalp knife by the nervous arm of a mountaineer was no baby blow, and seldom failed to strike home - up to the "Green River" on the blade." 12

In Wah-to-Yah and the Taos Trail, Lewis H. Gerrard's mountain men, Louy Simonds and Long Hatcher, are reminiscing.

"Mind the time we took Pawnee topknots away to the Platte?" Questioned Simonds. Hatcher replied, "Wagh! ef we didn't an' give an ogwh-ogwh longside that darned screechin', I'm a niggur. This child doesn't let an Injun count a coup alongside his cavyard always. They come mighty nigh rubbin' me out t'other side of Spanish peaks - woke up in the mornin' jist afore day, the devils yellin' like mad. I grabs my

Sharp Edges

knife, keels one, an' made for timber, with four of thar cussed arrows in my meatbag. The 'Patches took my beaver - five packs of teh prettiest in the mountains - an' two mules, but my traps was hid in the creek. Sez I, hyar's a gone coon if they keep my gun, so I follers thar trail an' at night crawls into camp, an' socks my big knife up to the Green River, first dig." 13

Despite the fact that these were novels, they are considered authentic representations of a mountain man's way of life.

Whether a knife was used as a tool, eating utensil, weapon, or skinning knife, it was important to a mountain man, and he often endowed it with a personality, and depended upon it as much or more than he did his companions. Woe to an Indian who stole a favorite knife, it might be his last theft. A lost knife would cause the party to call a halt, while the owner carefully backtracked until the knife was found or given up on as hopelessly lost. It didn't matter if the knives came from the factories of Sheffield, on the banks of the Green River in Massachusetts, or from the mountain man's own hand. It was source of pride, and invaluable tool, and a worthy companion.

Chapter 6
Knives of the Buffalo Skinners

When the white men first came to the Western part of the U.S., the vast herds of Buffalo astounded the explorers. Ernest Thompson Seton estimated the numbers to be around thirty million. Lewis and Clark observed, I do not think I exagerate when I esimate the number of Buffaloe which could be compre(hend)ed at one view to amount to 3000...." 1 One early white man said, "The ground seemed to be covered with a brown mantle of fur." 2 The first explorers took a few buffalo here and there to eat, or for robes, but it wasn't until the government was trying to eliminate the Indian threat from the plains that the buffalo slaughter got underway. Knowing that the Indians depended upon the buffalo for food, clothing, and material for the tepees, and utensils, General Phil Sheridan, in 1875, hearing that the Texas State Legislature wanted to pass a law to protect the buffalo, chided them, saying, "Let them kill, skin and sell until the buffalo is exterminated, as it is the only way to bring lasting peace and allow civilization to advance." 3 Colonel Richard Irving Dodge, in 1867, said, "Kill every buffalo you can. Every buffalo dead is an Indian gone." 4 This edict, and the fact that buffalo hides would bring from $2-$4 a piece, contributed to the decline of the vast herds, with over five million bufffalos being killed for their robes between the years 1872 and 1874, the height of the slaughter. The ten years between 1870 and 1880 was all it took for whites, Indians and half-breeds to wipe out the vast herds of buffalo that roamed the plains.

It seemed as if there would be buffalo forever. In 1872, the west went buffalo wild; everyone was chasing buffalo. In fact, when John Jacobs and John Poe set out as partners in buffalo hunting, one said, "We expected to be buffalo hunters all our lives." 6 Around

Sharp Edges

10,000 men were hunting buffalo, chasing the hides that were worth at the first of the year, $3.50, but, as the market became flooded, dropped to $.25. As people went broke, and went out, the price crept back up, to a high of $2.00 per hide.

Frank Mayer, who, for over a decade was a buffalo runner, said: "When I went into business, I sat down and figured that I was indeed one of fortunes children. Just think! There were 20,000,000 buffalo, each worth at least $3.00 - $60,000,000. At the very outside cartridges cost 25 cents each, so every time I fired I got my investment back twelve times over. I could kill a hundred a day, $300 gross, or couting everything, $200 net profit a day. ... We never killed all the buff we could, but only as many as our skinners could handle. Every outfit had its quota, which was determined by the ambition and the number of the skinners. My regular quota was twenty-five a day, but on days when my crew wasn't tired, I sometimes would run this up to 50 or even 60. But there I stopped; no matter how plentiful the buff were. Killing more than we could use would waste buff, which wasn't important; it also would waste ammunition, which was." 6

In the book, Heads, Hides and Horns, it says, "Men went out in small groups. Those who shot well did the hunting - the hunters. Others learned to skin the carcass and butcher it - the skinners." 7

Many men who later became famous for other exploits were, at one time, buffalo hunters, Wild Bill Hickok, Buffalo Bill, Pat Garrett, to name but a few. The rifles also went down in history, the Sharps, Winchesters, Springfields and Remingtons. But the men who did the work, the skinners, and their knives, have been an almost forgotten part of history. To have hides, the buffalo had to be skinned. It was hard, dirty work, requiring lots of sharp, rugged knives. The men who made history were the shooters, the romance of hunting the buffalo was what the public wanted, not the dirty work of skinning.

The hunter, or shooter, could down several buffalo in a day. Tom Nickson, a buffalo hunter, held the unofficial record for a one-day kill of 120 buffalo shot in forty minutes. John Cook killed eighty-eight in one stand. Colonel Dodge once counted one hundred and twelve carcasses within a semi-circle, "all of which had been killed by one man from the same spot, and in less than three-quarters of an hour." 8

But, for market hide hunters, it paid to only shoot as many buffalo as your skinners could take care of in one day, as buffalo left over night in warm weather began to swell, and those left to bake in the sun for four or five hours caused the hide to harden, and it was nearly impossible to remove. Such baked hides were weak, and would not bring full market value. On winter hunts, dead buffalo left over night froze, and the hides could not be taken, or wolves mangled the hide. Still, many times the hunters shot more buffalo than the skinners could handle, and wasted both the buffalo and the hide. Between the years 1872 and 1873, Colonel Dodge estimated that from 1/4 to 1/3 of the hides from dead buffalo actually reached the markets.

A buffalo hunters outfit usually consisted of one or two hunters, who were usually also the owners of the outfit, two to three skinners, paid about $.05 per hide, a cook who also helped stretch the hides, a light wagon to take the outfit into the wilderness, and bring the hides back, chuckwagon, guns, powder primers, lead shells, and, of course, skinning knives. The fare was meat, beans, hardtack, and coffee. Tableware consisted of plates and cups. As one wag put it, "The fastidious could impale their food on their skinning knives, the democrats used their fingers." 9

The hide hunter himself made the most money, although the cost of the outfit was not cheap, running around $1000 or over. Wyatt Earp, who later gained fame as a frontier marshal, felt that most outfits were badly run and un-businesslike. He felt that the hunter often employed skinners when he could easily skin himself, as most shooters retired to the wagon after the killing was done, and left the skinners do the work. It was tradition, "What, touch a skinning knife? Not on your life."

In April 1872, Earp took a shotgun on the buffalo range, and with one skinner, began hide hunting. "My lowest score for a single day was eighteen buffalos, my highest, twenty-seven. As I never shot but one stand a day, that meant twenty to thirty-five dollars apiece for the skinner and myself." 10. Earp joined in the skinning, and found why tradition forbade it; it was hard, dirty work. But he cleared more than $2500 for a months work.

The skinners made about average for the times, on a good day one skinner could skin about 50 animals, pay was either on a per

Sharp Edges

A modern reproduction of a Green River Skinner rests on a buffalo skull. (Author's collection, knife from Crazy Crow Trading Company.)

Vannoy

head skinned basics, from $.05 up to as high as $.30, or a flat rate of $50.00 per month, still better than the cowboys, who worked for $1.00 per day and found. Still, it wasn't an easy job for the money, and, due to the blood and dirt that was a part of the job, the skinner was often a persona non grata in saloons until he was bathed and laundered.

To skin an animal as big as a buffalo, which can weight up to a ton, required good knives. When buffalo hunting was just a matter of dropping a few here and there for a stew pot, any knife could handle the job, usually large bowie knives or butcher knives. Lieutenant George Brewerton, along the Santa Fe Trail, found that skinning wasn't all that easy. He killed a buff, and, "drew his Bowie knife - and for thirty minutes, "labored...pulling, slashing, and hacking, right and left at the huge carcass.... until I blunted the knife, lost my temper...." 11. As the hides became valuable, greater care was taken to skin them without damage to the hide.

William T. Hornaday described the professional still hunter, and the knives he used on the prairie. "Each man hunted separately, and skinned all the animals his rifle brought down. ...At his side, depending from his belt, hung his "hunter's companion", a flat leather scabbard, containing a ripping knife, a skinning knife, and a butcher's steel upon which to sharpen them." 12

Few of these have been preserved. One that was preserved for many years, but now seems to be lost, was in the Yellowstone National Park Museum. I talked to the curator there, and he found nothing about it, and assumed that it had either been lost, or had been in such bad shape that they disposed of it. A description of the scabbard was given by a park naturalist and quoted in the book, Firearms, Traps and Tools of the Mountain Men, "It is a three pocketed sheath now containing one knife, and was found beside a buffalo carcass in eastern Montana in 1884. The other knife and steel have never been in our possession, nor do we know that they were ever found. The sheath measures 5" by 11" and is made of tanned leather. The pockets measure 6 1/2, by 1 7/8, 6 1/2 by 1", and 6 1/2 by 2 1/4". The belt slits are three inches long. The knife is about 10 inches long. The rusted 6" inch steel blade extends into the 4" wooden handle. There are no identifying marks." 13

Many skinning and ripping knives were homemade knives,

Sharp Edges

such as one skinner that was made from a circular saw blade, but as the demand for hides grew, so did the demand for knives, and manufactures began to make knives to be sent West for use in the skinners outfits.

Many were made on the plains as necessity demanded, such as we see in the book, *Bowie Knife*, "Makers of 'bowie knives' swarmed into the plains country of the West during the great buffalo-slaughtering era of the 1870's. The knife-trade flourished, with more than ten thousand hunters turning over to the "skinners" tens of thousands of animals at a time. These "wandering blacksmiths" carried portable forges and used buffalo chips for fuel." 14

In 1840, six hundred half-breed Canadian buffalo hunters assembled in Pembine, Manitoba, and had in their possession 1,240 skinning knives.

Also, in 1840 Pierre Chouteau ordered for his winter trade with the Indians, for buffalo robes and other furs, "six thousand pairs of French blankets; three hundred "North West English guns." which cost him $5.62 1/2 each; three hundred dozen butcher knives..." 15

Two names that are almost synonymous with the buffalo skinners are the Green River Skinners and I. Wilson Skinners. These knives, of which the Green River, marketed by J. Russell and Company, in Connecticut, was the first, and I. Wilson simply a copy from Sheffield, England, were curved skinning knives, preferred by both buffalo hunters and mountain men. The large ripping knives were often referred to as Bowie knives, and many were shipped west from the factories at Sheffield, Green River Works, and Lamson and Goodnow makers.

Tom Bird, a Texas ranger who made history by taking his wife into the buffalo hunting camp, outfitted out of Fort Belknap, Texas. Mrs. Bird describes her impressions on the hunt, and wrote about the outfit. "A large buffalo gun, Sharps 45, weighed 16 pounds...two I Wilson skinning knives, one buoy knife, and a large steel..." 17

One Mr. McNaney, who appeared in Hornaday's account of the American Bison, described his outfit, which consisted of the usual equipment and 60 Wilson skinning knives, (probably I. Wilson.) three butcher steels, and 1 portable grindstone to keep the knives sharp.

Vannoy

A butcher knife of the type that may have been used by the buffalo skinners. (Courtesy of Crazy Crow Trading Company, Pottsboro, Texas.

Although a modern reproduction, this was a very common style of knife that could have been marketed as a 'ripping knife.' (Author's Collection)

Sharp Edges

Skinners carried a steel to do quick touch up jobs on the knives, and usually carried several knives with them.

Buffalo could be skinned in various ways, and it was said that a person could tell which outfit was hunting by the way the carcasses had been skinned.

In his book, the Great Buffalo Hunt, Wayne Gard describes the skinning process. "Ordinarily, using a pointed ripping knife, sharp as a razor, one man slide the hide from beneath the lower jaw, along the neck and down the belly to the tail. Then he ripped the hide down the inside of each leg. Next, the skinners with a crescent shaped by less pointed skinning knife, (Green River or I Wilson.) cut around the neck, taking the ears but leaving the skin on the head, and loosening the hide from the carcass. Finally, with a rope noosed around the skin of the buffalo's neck and ears, a horse pulled off the hide." 18

William T. Hornaday, who interviewed and corresponded with buffalo hunters during the 1870's and 1880's, gives a description of the skinning process. After the carcass was rolled on it's back, the sharp pointed 'ripping knife' was used to, "make all the opening cuts in the skin. Each leg was girdled to the bone, about 8 inches above the hoof, and the skin of the leg ripped open from that point along the inside to the median line of the body (belly). A long straight cut was then made along the middle of the breast and abdomen, from the root of the tail to the chin... The opening cuts having been made, the broad, (curved) skinning knife was used to detach the skin from the body in the shortest possible time. The tail was always skinned and left on the hide." 19

"The fur-buyers had taught the hunters, with the potent argument of hard cash, that a robe carefully taken off, stretched, and kept reasonably free from blood and dirt, was worth more money in the market than one taken off in a slovenly manner. After 1880, buffalo on the northern range were skinned with considerable care, and amongst the robe hunters not one was allowed to become a loss when it was possible to prevent it. Every full sized cow robe was considered equal to $3.50 in hard cash, and treated accordingly. The hunter, or skinner, always stretched every robe out on the ground to it's fullest extent while it was yet warm, and cut the initials of his employer in the thin subcutaneous muscle which always adhered to

Vannoy

the inside of the skin. A warm skin is very elastic, and when stretched upon the ground the hair holds it's shape until it either dries or freezes, and so retains its full size." 20

Once stretched, small holes were cut through the hide around the outer edge, and sharpened pegs about six inches long were driven through the holes to hold the hide to its proper shape. Once dry, the hides were folded and stacked. When the pile of hides was about eight feet high, rawhide strings were cut from a green hide, that is, one that wasn't dried, and threaded through the peg holes in the corners of the dried hides, and pulled tightly. The pile was then ready for the buyer.

The hide hunters, trying to stack as many hides as possible in a short amount of time, seldom worried about fleshing the hides, except to make sure that the largest pieces of tissue were removed.

A few of the skinners names went down in history, but most are forgotten. Bill Hillman, who skinned seventy carcasses between breakfast and 4 p.m., went down as an almost mythical champion. Sam Carr was a lone hunter, who shot and skinned the animals himself, collecting all the profits. It was reported he sometimes brought in thirty-five to forty hides per day. Johnny Cook, who later became a buffalo hunter, worked as a skinner for Charlie Hart. But most have been forgotten. As have the knives, the I. Wilsons, the Green Rivers, the Sheffield Bowies, that played a part in the winning of the western frontier.

Chapter 7
Knives of the Gold Fields

Gold! That glittering yellow metal that excites the imagination and has probably brought about more exploration than anything else in history. America was, in part, discovered for it's gold by the Spanish, who heard of the fabled Seven Cities of Gold, and many died searching for them. But more recent history also embraces the golden metal.

California, Montana, South Dakota and Alaska were all gold country at one time, and the discovery of gold hastened settlement and statehood to many states, especially California during the '49 gold rush.

The '49ers of California and later the sourdoughs of Alaska left their mark on our culture, history and literature.

As in any culture, such as the Indians, colonists, or cowboys, the gold fields developed a style of knives best suited for the tastes and needs of the day. In Bernard Levine's book, Knifemakers of Old San Francisco, he writes; "Miners used their knives every day to convert antelope, deer, elk, bear, cattle, duck, fish, or rabbit into dinner around the campfire. And at the diggings, "Many miners frequently pick gold out of the crevices of rocks with their butcher knives, in pieces from one to six ounces." 1 They even developed a name for the technique, crevicing. One man, Edward Gould Buffum, a lieutenant in the U.S. Army volunteers, wrote in 1848. "I shall never forget the delight with which I struck and worked out a crevice...It appeared to be filled with a hard, bluish clay and gravel, which I took out with my knife, and there at the bottom, strewn along the whole length of the rock, was bright yellow gold... When my eyes were sufficiently feasted I scooped it out with the point of my knife..." 2

Vannoy

In a letter from Col. R.B. Mason and Lt. W.T. Sherman to the War Department, August 17, 1848 he says that knives were a dependable sidearm, "Whether or not he carried a pistol, every Forty-Niner carried a knife - butcher knife, Bowie knife, or dirk - with him wherever he went. A man in a tight corner, with his life or treasure at stake, knew that his knife was sure to be loaded, and could never fail to fire." 3

One painting in the California Historical society shows a forty-niner with four knives residing in his pocket, two with blades up, one resembles a clip-pointed bowie and the other a spear pointed dagger style knife, and one looks to be a small sword or a Scottish dirk, and the other has a curved handle like the top of a cane. 4

Gold was reported to be easy to come by in California, and it was rumored that all a man had to do was pick it up. Some came west with no more than a jackknife of a spoon to dig for gold.

Knifemakers, seeing the gold seekers used and purchased knives, gave California the distinction of having its name inscribed on more Bowie knives than any other state. For the up and coming gold miner, knives could be purchased bearing such sediments, as "California Knife," Chevalier's California Knife," "I Can Dig Gold From Quartz" and "For the Gold Searchers Protection." To name but a few of the sediments inscribed on knives.

As one writer, H.R. Halper wrote in the mid-1850's, "By calculation based on fair estimates I learn that since California opened her mines to the world she has invested upwards of six million dollars in Bowie knives and pistols." 5

Probably no where else in history, since the first settlers came from Germany, Ireland, Scotland, and England to settle the Eastern part of the U.S., have so many immigrates came into the States as they did during the '49 gold rush. Mexican's, of course, were already here, and had pretty much claimed California. Then came the Yankees from the Eastern and Midwestern states and territories. Miners came from Ireland, Chile, Wales, Germany, Australia, Scotland, China, Peru and France looking for the glittering metal, hoping for instant wealth. Many found it, although few actually found it in gold. Much of the money made was by enterprising merchants, who found it was easier to sell equipment to the miners than actually mine the gold.

Sharp Edges

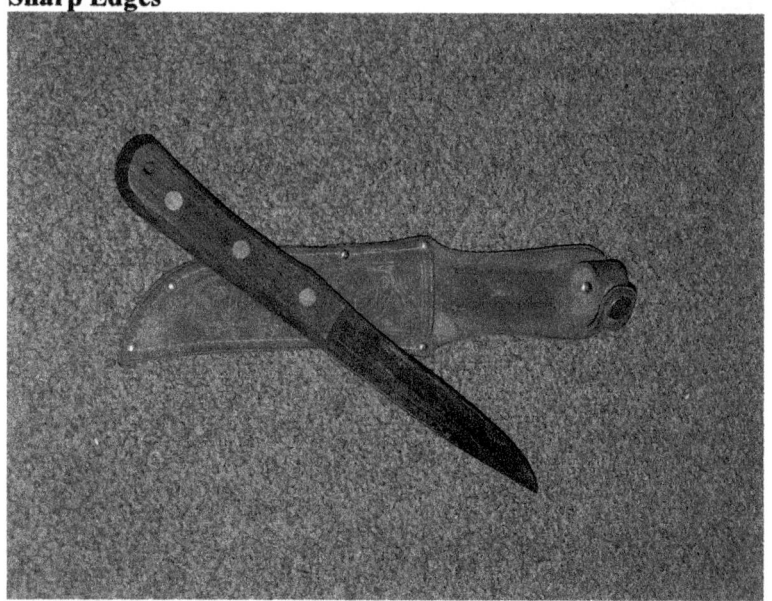

A butcher knife, easy to find, cheap and well-made, these were undoubtedly used more often for camp chores and for whatever came up than any of the more famous knives.
Authors Collection

Vannoy

Many miners were spirited men looking for adventure, but also the lawless, very often criminals from other countries, eager to try their luck and escape prosecution.

One man describes such a group of ruffians, from South Wales. "Dressed in discolored red shirts, their ugly and dirty faces peering with cunning impudence from beneath flaming red flannel caps, which, from their shape, might be camp pudding bags; around their waists circled greasy leathern belts, in which revolved, at east, a wooden-handled sheath-knife used to blood of man or beast." 6

The Chinese developed their own system of law an order among themselves. Persecuted by nearly everyone else, the Chinese lived among themselves. In San Francisco, with the flames undoubtedly fanned by the Whites, rival tongs, or groups of Chinese, declared war. "There was one stated battle between tongs, encouraged by the Whites, which kept the blacksmiths busy for weeks manufacturing breastplates, helmets and spears...They went at it with hatchets, knives, maces and spears. A few of them had pistols but the oriental idea of manslaughter is not just to make a pop and see someone fall over but to produce a good loud thunk manually, audible to honorable ancestors."

"Ever since the gold rush, Chinese merchants in Sand Francisco had imported distinctive Chinese vegetable cleavers, meat cleavers, daggers, double daggers and heavy bladed swords. Chinese smiths working in the mining districts of California, and some of them made knives." 8 Will & Finck also made knives for the Chinese trade, and at least one of these survives. It has a walrus ivory handle and well-forged blade.

In a brief article in an old newspaper, a few years after the '49 rush, 1860, it reads, "Cutting Affray Between Frenchmen and Chinese" There was a dispute over a wash bill in a Chinese laundry, and the Chinese inflicted several severe wounds. "Ordinarily, the Chinese are more sinned against than sinning, but lately the Johns are getting to be right valiant in the used of knives and slung shots," the writer states.

The Mexican's were a little higher on the pecking order in the camps than were the Chinese, most Mexican's stayed on their rancheros in the South, and didn't invade the miners territory of San Francisco. A few did, "They were an adventurous class of younger

Sharp Edges

men who hated the Anglo-Saxon intruders; they were at once dissolute and indolent; they were the first procurers of the northern settlements because they could manage a certain supply of women from the south; they were light-fingered and they fought with knives." 10. According to one book, the only woman hung in the mining camps on record; "She was, of course, a Mexican. A Scotsman in Downieville took too much at the bar one night ...and decided to visit a Mexican lady of the community...the sonora's husband or friend had no objection to the visit, but the senora stabbed the Scot neatly in the heart." 11

The people of the town condoned the hanging, and speculation has it that she was not popular. "Perhaps she had tantrums and had used a knife before; " 12.

Mexican people, of course, have used knives for centuries. One entertainment in Mexico and Old California was roping a grizzly bear, tying it securely to a tree, and then killing it with a knife.

Levine's guide to knives shows two examples of Mexican knives. One, very ornate, with etching on the blade and a carved stag eagle head handle, looks like a typical American Bowie knife, with the guard, and the clip pointed blade. It is 14 inches long. Another example is a Mexican utility knife, which looks like a very large, 12 inches long, skinning knife.

In fact, in the William R. Williamson article in a Blade Magazine, titled "The Spanish Notch", Mr. Williamson writes: "The Bowie knife was fathered by that breed of fighting and hunting knife born in the Mediterranean area of Spain, Italy and the south of France." 13 The knives, Spanish Dirks and Spanish Daggers, became the forerunners of the Mexican knives, and the forefathers of the American Bowie.

In another Blade Magazine, Vic Walker writes of the Mexican Bowie: "The Mexican Campesino's sheath knife and machete are indispensable to his daily existence. The knife butchers his animals, mends his huaraches, picks his teeth and trims his toenails. His machete clears brush, cuts hay, trims poles and chops wood. Either may double as a weapon. Such a vigilant companion, in the eyes of its owner, must bear some sort of soul, thus is deserving of its own name. No different from the medieval knight with his "Singing Sword" or the frontiersman with his "Old Betsy" rifle." 14

Vannoy

Knives of different cultures came together in California, as did the different cultures that used them. Later gold rushes were not to see such a wealth of diverse cultures coming together after a common goal, as did the rush of '49.

As many of the miners grew wealthy, (and many went broke), they began to look for ways to spend the wealth, and outfit them selves in a style becoming a successful gold miner. They carried gold watches; gold headed canes, and purchased gold jewelry for wives and mistresses. Their aesthetic taste carried over to their knives. Until 1852, knives had to be ordered from Europe, or from Eastern cutlers such as J. Russell. According to John Hittell, Commerce and Industries of the Pacific Coast 1882, quoted in Levine's book says of Hugh McConnell, first known established cutler in San Francisco, "...in 1852 made butcher knives and bowie knives, the latter being of excellent temper and mounted with silver, or even gold, in such manner that a knife sold for $100 or more." 15 This price rivals today's prices paid to knife makers for collection quality custom knives. But, a man with gold in his pocket, and a producing claim, didn't care about cost. If he wanted it, he bought it, paying in gold.

"At the first Exhibition of the Mechanics Institute of San Francisco in 1857, Hugh McConnell was awarded a diploma for a case of fine cutlery of his manufacture. In the case was displayed, "A hunting knife, with heavy blade, very beautifully finished." Frederick Kesmodel, in the same exhibit, won a bronze medal for a case of cutlery of his manufacture." 16

But such knives were for the rich. Most miners made enough to keep alive, and some didn't make that before giving up and returning home or finding it easier to obtain gold by selling something someone wanted, rather than break their backs digging for it.

During the first few years in California, when gold was plentiful, knives were mostly used as tools for hunting and camp chores, as most miners were too intend on digging gold to waste time in fighting, and most mining camps had strict rules governing their miners to keep the peace. And, there seemed to be enough gold for everyone. But, as claims played out, and more people moved in, more ruffians and people of ill-repute began to frequent the camps. Knives became not only a tool, but also a lethal weapon, and a man's life might depend on his skill with his Bowie knife, or dirk.

Sharp Edges

Granville Stuart, who's writings were published in 1925, prospected for gold from California to Montana from 1852-1864 mentioned knives off and on throughout his journals. One interesting incident happened in California. He and his partners found pay dirt near Dog Town, and, having neither pencil or paper with which to put up a notice that they were claiming the ground, went back to the cabin, intending to put up a claim notice the next morning. The next day, Granville writes, his brother James and their friend decided to wash clothes instead, saying there was no danger of anyone finding the claim anyway.

It was a costly washing for, ".... when we went to the mine on Monday morning, Lo and behold! There was Tom Neal...." Tom had ridden in Sunday, and, "seeing where we had scratched out the place in the bank, and that convenient old case knife laying right there, he, as we had done, picked it up and began scratching in the place where we had dug."

Neal put in his claim on the diggings, and Stuart continues, "Now, if we had taken a little trouble to cover up the place where we had dug, with dry dirt and thrown that tell-tale old knife away, Tom and party would doubtless have passed on, as he had often done before, and done no scratching." 17 So, in a way, the old caseknife worked to betray a claim to another prospector.

In Colorado, during the gold strike of 1859, one man, George Jackson, related to a newspaper reporter, ".... If I only had a pick and a pan instead of a hunting knife and the cup, I could dig a sackful of the yellow stuff and carry it down to the boys." Later he writes in his journal, on Jan 8th "Dug and panned gold today until my belt knife was worn out, so will have to use my skinning knife. I have about an ounce of gold, so will try to get back in the spring." 18

Although there were rich diggings, as the miners called them, many miners echoed the sediment found scratched with a knife on the bottom of a tin cup in British Columbia, during the gold rush there in 1860. "Dying of starvation - Rose."

In Alaska, during the gold rush just before the turn of the century, knives were used for survival in the most primitive sense, not man against man, but man against his most formidable enemy, nature itself. Although seldom mentioned in writings, a knife was an important tool to the gold miners in Alaska. A man without a knife

Vannoy

A common butcher knife such was used throughout the gold fields for everything from digging gold out of rocks to cutting a steak off a beef or a deer. Courtesy of Crazy Crow Trading Company, Pottsboro, Texas.

Sharp Edges
on the trail was nearly helpless, even if he killed game, he would have no way of gutting, skinning or butchering it. Knives were used to repair dog harnesses, to cut branches for firewood and bedding, and numerous other uses around camp. In the book, Sourdough, the story of Slim Williams, by Richard Morenus, he says of the hopefuls for gold, "Some men had no outfits at all except the clothing they wore, a little food, a gun, and a knife." 19

In the book, Sourdough Sagas, Herbert L. Heller, he quotes from the Chicago Daily Tribune-Tribune Extra Klondike Edition, 1898, about the outfit needed for one man for one year of diggings.

Along with clothing, which included "5 yards mosquito netting, 3 suits of heavy underware," mackinaw coat and pants, (2 pair), wool socks and gloves; Groceries, including 200 lbs of bacon, 300 lbs flour 25 lbs each apples, peaches, apricots, and pitted prunes, as well as coffee, sugar, beans, yeast and matches; there was also the Hardware and Camp Outfit: "One pair ice creepers, one sheath knife and sheath, 2 miners' shovels, 1 spool wire, 4 sail needles, 2 gold pans... half dozen 8-inch flat files, 1 handled ax and 2 handles......1 set knives and forks, (six each), fry pan, coffee mill, gold scale, sled, tent, stove and 1 box candles."

Armament included: "One repeating rifle, 30-30 with reloading tools and 100 rounds of brass shell cartridges, 1 large hunting knife, and an assortment of fishing tackle."

The weight of the entire outfit was nearly 1500 pounds, and the cost was nearly $300.00.

In the Chicago Daily Tribune in March of 1898, there was an ad from AM Rothschild & Co, on State and Van Buren Streets. They advertised "Sharp reductions in IXL pocketknives. IXL & Non XL knives - we have just received 1,500 of the highest grade Sheffield English made goods-all warrented-nothing better made - in stag, ivory, buffalo & mother of pearl handles - 1,2,3,and 4 blades - values up to $2.50- all go at 1/2 value - the chance will not come again - $2.50 knives at $1.25, $2.00 knives at $1.00, $1.50 knives at $.75, $1.00 knives at $.50, $.50 knives at $.25." 21

Jack London, author, was one of the many adventurers who caught the gold excitement and headed for the Yukon. While there, he made copious notes about what he did and saw among the miners, and, later, was to make more money off the stories about the gold rush

Vannoy
than most sourdoughs did off the gold they panned. Although fiction, many of his stories were eagerly awaited by the sourdoughs, as they felt that London gave them the only authentic stories of the their lives. Knives often played an important part in London's work. In one short story, *The Son of the Wolf*, 'Scruff' Mackenzie, a miner in search of a wife who finds one in an Indian village. After living with the Indians for a time, he convinces the girl to marry him, and she, "...took from her sewing bag a moose hide sheath, brave with bright beadwork, fantastically designed. She drew his great hunting-knife, gazed reverently along the keen edge, half tempted to try it with her thumb, and shot it into place in its new home. Then she slipped the sheath along the belt to its customary resting-place, just above the hip."

The woman was a chief's daughter, and he refused Mackenzie's request for the girl. A fight broke out, and one of the Indian, The Bear, "came to the center of the battleground, a long naked hunting-knife of Russian make in his hand." Mackenize draws his knife, "Not only in reach and stature had the Bear the advantage of him, but his blade was longer by a good two inches. "Scruff" Mackenzie had looked into the eyes of men before, and he knew it was a man who stood against him; yet he quickened to the glint of light on the steel, to the dominant pulse of his race." Mackenize finally gets the better of Bear, just in time to duck an arrow directed by the Shaman that killed Bear. "Mackenzie's knife leaped short in the air. He caught the heavy blade by the point. There was a flash of light as it spanned the fire. The Shaman, the hilt alone appearing without his throat, swayed a moment and pitched forward into the glowing embers." 22 Mackenzie won his fair lady, and took he down the trail with him. But most miners' lives were not so exciting, and fewer real life fights involved knives then were recorded in fiction.

John Todt, was a knife maker in San Francisco from 1880 until 1906, after the San Francisco fire. He made high quality bowie knives. His son, Alfred Todt, helped him in his business. In Knifemakers of Old San Francisco, an interesting story is related, "Alfred Todt, Jr. is retired now. He recalls that about a dozen years ago, an old, old man tottered into his locksmith shop on Second Street and asked to see John Todt. He was disappointed to learn that the old knife maker had been dead for fifty years. He said that when he was

Sharp Edges

young, John Todt had made him a pair of bowie knives. He had taken the knives with him when he went up north to Alaska in 1898. Later, he had joined the Royal Canadian Mounted Police. He had, so he recounted, broken one of the knives, "settling" a barroom fight somewhere in the Northwest. He still had the other knife, and he had saved the pieces of the broken one. Would Mr. Todt like to see them? He certainly would. The old man tottered out, promising to return soon. He never came back. Perhaps he died; perhaps he just forgot." 23 Levine's book was copyrighted in 1977, so the above incident must have happened in the mid-1960's. Quite a testament to a Todt knife.

Other than the knives made in San Francisco, makers of knives during the gold rushes is a matter of speculation. Nearly every cutler that was in business at the time would have been represented in the gold fields, including Green River Knives, Sheffield Knives, Lamson & Goodnow, and John Chevalier. These cutlers were in business at the time of the '49 gold rush, and many stayed in business up until the turn of the century.

These firms made hunting knives, skinning knives, and bowie knives to outfit the miners on their quest for the gold metal.

In Montana, after the end of the I World War, several men set up a hydraulic system in Confederate Gulch, so thirty-five miles southeast of Helena. They found gold, also a collection of bullets, coins, knives, pistols and guns left since the boom of 1864. Rusted and pitted ghosts of an era when the cry "gold" fired men's imaginations and the lure of the shining metal glittered in their eyes.

Chapter 8
Knives of the Civil War

Probably more has been written about the Civil war than about any other war in the history of man. For one thing it was fought on American soil, and the enemy was not some foreign army, but an army of friends, neighbors, occasionally brothers fought against each other as loyalties were divided, and the country itself was split into warring factions.

Articles and books by the score have been written on the people, the generals, the battles, the causes, and the rifles used. But very little is written about the knives the troops used during the conflict.

Swords have taken the spotlight, with more reference made to them in most research information than to the knives. Bayonets, as well, received their share of the spotlight, and historians often forget that in the South, many of what were called bayonets actually were bowie knives with bayonet rings fixed to the knife so it could be attached to the rifle. In addition to the officers' swords, and the bayonets, although not regulation, most of the soldiers carried some type of sheath knife, either a Bowie, toothpick, or simply a good stout hunting knife.

The bowie knife, made popular after the Alamo by Jim Bowie's fame, became "the knife" for adventurers, hunters, soldiers, and anyone wanting a big, stout survival type knife. Many of these saw used during the Mexican-American war. It the book, Military Dress of North America, the First Mississippi Regiment Rifleman is described. "This unit saved the honour of the American volunteers at Buena Vista by obeying the order to "Stand Fast!" of their wounded Colonel Jefferson Davis;..no bayonets were issued and

Sharp Edges

A Confederate D-Guard Bowie Knife. Courtesy of Crazy Crow Trading Company, Pottsboro, TX.

Vannoy

most volunteers carried the murderous Bowie or Arkansas Knives instead." It said of the Texas Rangers, "Arms consisted of privately owned flintlock rifles, huge Bowie knives, the occasional captured Mexican sabre, lariats, and, invariably, a terrifying array of pistols." 1

Twenty years later, the conflict between the Northern and Southern states broke out.

The South was a rural, agricultural economy, while the North was moving rapidly towards industrialization, and an economy based on manufacturing.

In a newspaper article from the Charleston Mercury, in Feb. of 1862, the writer bemoans the fact that the North has, "Factories for the manufacture of cannon, rifles, sabers, bayonets, and ammunition of every description, are in full
operation at the North during the whole twenty four hours of every day." 2 He also mentioned that Northern agents were being sent to Europe to procure the best possible arms.

The Southern troops often had to rely on older weaponry, or stolen goods. One soldier remarked, "Everything was branded US except ourselves." 3

From the book, Civil War Collectors Encyclopedia, Francis Lord, Stackpole Books, Harrisburg, PA. "Early in the war many volunteers on both sides were presented with bowie knives of various patterns and lengths. They were more popular with the Southern troops than with Northern, but even the Federals used them." 4

The town of Ashby, Shelburne Falls, and other Massachusetts towns presented every one of its residents with a bowie knife when he enlisted, and Company C of the 1st Georgia Infantry from Cass County were known as the "The Bowie Knife Boys."

At the start of the war a local pastor made a speech in donating bowie knives to a group of Federal volunteers. He held up one of these knives before a "tearful and shuddering audience," and exhorted the men to, "Strike 'til the last armed foe expires."

However, sad ends for the knives, as they were used for nothing more violent, "except to saw slices of bacon, chop off chickens' heads, or cut sticks to hold the coffee pots over the fire." 5

In the book, The American Civil War, by Earl Schenck Miers, it tells of the Missouri Rebels, a group of frontiersmen knocked into army shape during the first few months of the war.

Sharp Edges
Although these men knew nothing of military discipline, they were hunters by necessity, who knew "how to handle a gun or a Bowie knife (which, in their idiom, was invariably an "Arkansas toothpick")" They may have looked a little ridiculous to seasoned soldiers, but they had the intelligence, bravery, cunning, and other skills that made them fierce fighters. They could live off the land, and were experts at the guerrilla warfare." 6

According to Bernard Levine, in his collectors guide to knives, "Guide to Knives and their Values," he has a brief paragraph about Civil War knives, mainly bowies. "A decade after the gold rush, with the start of the Civil War, demand surged again for bowie knives. They had long been popular in the South, and this inspired some southern politicians, particularly Governor Joseph E. Brown of Georgia, to order large quantities of massive locally made bowie knives, often with "D-guards," for issue to Confederate troops and home guards. In the field, the troops found those big weapons not merely useless, but an actual encumbrance, and threw them away." 7

This could have been the knives that the State of Georgia purchased in 1862, ordering a total of 4,909 bowie knives from hundreds of different makers. These were, "side knives, with eighteen-inch blade, weighing about three pounds." 8 The State paid $4.60 for each knife complete with belt and scabbard.

"Officers and men on both sides of the conflict often carried conventional sized bowie knives and dirks, (small daggers). Most of these were cheap and gaudy Sheffield knives, because only senior officers could afford the $10 to $300 for a made-to-order bowie from an American cutler or surgical instrument maker." 9

Cutlers that manufactured knives during the conflict for the Northern troops included Ames Manufacturing, Cabotville, Mass, Brown and Tetley, Pittsburgh, John Chevalier, New York, and William Rogers Manufacturing Co, Hartford, Conn. to name a few.

Confederate suppliers included Peter W. Kraft, Columbia, SC, who advertised in Jan of 1861 in a Richmond paper, "Bowie knives, find English, French and German double guns....." R.J. Hughes, Delivered 1,294 Bowie knives on April 16, 1862, and 1,103 belts on the same date. Delivered 175 Bowie knives on May 10., O.S. Haynes, Georgia, Delivered 49 Bowie knives in April of 1862, Gitter

Vannoy
and Moss of Memphis, Tennessee, ran and ad Dec. 12, 1861, "making Army cutlery of all kinds." All who wanted a good sword or knife were invited to call. Georgia seems to be the chief knife state, with many makers given credit for supplying the Georgia troops with knives. 10

The bowie had a following on both sides of the conflict, and it was the most used and most often found in references from the period. Another knife sometimes used was the dagger, a double-edged pointed weapon that was good only for close fighting. In his observation of Death on the Battlefield, Captain Henry Blake, of the 11th Massachusetts Volunteers, after the battle of Williamsburg, wrote, "The brief experience of a single engagement satisfied men of the uselessness of revolvers or dirks for the purposes of war, and they disappeared from both armies." 11

In the Petersen book, Daggers and Fighting Knives, there are illustrations of some of the various knives used during the war. One was a Sheffield bowie made by George Wostenhold and carried by a Union soldier. The grips are antler, and the knife is a typical bowie, with the long blade with the upswept point. Another was a large Confederate bowie, with an iron knuckle bow and a tinned iron sheath, and one is shown with an etched blade and a table cutlery type handle, again made in Sheffield.

One knife illustrated in Levin's book was an unmarked Georgia -type D-guard bowie, 20 3/4 inches overall, with a wood handle and steel guard. Brown and Tetley Company of Pittsburgh made another such knife, about 1855-1862. The blade alone is 20 1/4 inches long.

But most of the knives weren't that long, they were awkward and impractical to carry. The majority of bowie knives were more the large hunting knife size, with a blade of from 8 to a little over 12 inches, with the handle adding perhaps adding another 4 to six inches.

Many knives were home made, either by country blacksmiths or others who set themselves up as occasional knife makers. In American Knives, Petersen has photographs of three of these type knives. One was made from a file, with an iron guard, similar to those used by the Confederates during the war. Another knife used by the Confederates was found in Texas, with a heavy 9 1/4 inch blade with an antler handle.

Sharp Edges

In one book, it tells of the Confederate arms, "Often men turned out with items they had brought from home - shotguns or hunting rifles, crudely fashioned sabers, Bowie knives and every kind of pistol." 12 In an old photograph a confederate soldier is shown holding a rifle in one hand and a huge Bowie knife in the other.

In the August 1988 Blade magazine, in the Edges of the Past column, there appears a quote from an Arthur Fremantle, a British officer touring the Southern Army just before the battle of Gettysburg. "They were in the habit of wearing numerous revolvers and Bowie knives. General Lee mildly remarked, I think you will find an Enfield rifle, a bayonet, and sixty round of ammunition as much as you can conveniently carry in the way of arms." 13

In an article by Leo Huff, in the Arkansas Historical Quarterly, titled "The Military Board in Confederate Arkansas," there is this: "Also, the "Arkansas toothpick" or Bowie knife was a favorite weapon of the Arkansas troops, and a huge knife strapped on the belt seemed to be the badge of the soldier. The local blacksmiths were kept busy making Bowie knives from old files and other scrap iron. One company of Rangers carried large Bowie knives ranging from twenty-five to thirty inches in length.

"As the shortage of arms became increasingly serious, more people became intrigued with the idea of using bladed weapons as a substitute for firearms. One newspaper editor advised in the spring of 1862 that steel pikes could be made and mounted on an eight-foot long ashen staff for five dollars each." 14

Jimmy Lile, "The Arkansas Knifesmith" responded to my question about the Arkansas toothpick: "The Arkansas toothpick got its name during the Civil War when the availability of commercial knives from England and the North were shut off. At that time it became more necessary for the Confederate soldiers to make their own fighting tools. Every plantation had a blacksmith, some better than others, who made many knives that later became known as Bowie knives and the Arkansas toothpick. One very believable legend has it that the Arkansas regiment carried such knives into battle and became known as "those old long knife boys from Arkansas." 15

Confederate soldiers, with the shortage of arms, considered a bowie knife standard equipment, and referred to all sheath knives as

Vannoy

"bowies". In official talk, they were referred to as "side knives." Some states, such as Georgia, purchased large numbers of knives from various makers, but very few were marked with the markers stamp. Many mounted soldiers favored pocket- knives with hoof picks, in case the horse picked up a stone in its hoof.

In an article, *The Clank, Clash and Glitter of Steel*, part 1, "Virtually each Southerner carried a blade of edged steel. Cavalrymen sported sabers of diverse designs, while infantrymen boasted both bayonets and sheath knives for use at close quarters with the enemy. Johnny Reb marched away to war with an abiding faith in the lethal value of cold steel...."

Mr. Austerman goes on to say, "The Southern troops love affair with the blade took many forms, depending upon whether he marched or rode into battle, but the most common edged weapon was the knife." He then quotes from a Southern historian, "The Bowie knife fever ran high ... early in the war. No common soldier felt fully armed unless he had a knife in his belt. Many of the better knives were imported from Sheffield, England. Others were manufactured in bulk by New England cutlers, and in smaller quantities by Southern blacksmiths and iron workers."

Texans, wild and wooly from the frontier, felt naked without a large knife on their hip, possibly in reminiscence of Jim Bowie at the Alamo. The men in the 3rd Texas Cavalry carried knives, "heavy enough to cleave the skull of a mailed knight, helmet and all." 16

"Many, expecting terrific hand-to-hand encounters, carried revolvers, and even bowie knives." 17 The article is a compilation of Civil War writings from the people who were there.

During the battle of Pea Ridge, a bloody encounter occurred between a Missouri soldier and a Rebel, "found themselves climbing the same fence. Each was armed with Bowie knives." The Rebel challenged his enemy to combat. "The Missourian had more strength, but the rebel more skill......soon the former was covered with blood....he became desperate. The rebel made a stroke....became overbalanced.... The Missourian saw his chance. His blade, hurled through the air, fell with tremendous force on the rebels neck....nearly severing the head from the body."
Such was the legacy of the bowie knife. 18

In another description, written by Captain Henry Blake of the

Sharp Edges

11th Massachusetts Volunteers, about death on the battlefield, Captain Blake writes: "I noticed a number of the dead of the Union army had been mutilated by bowie-knives, made of large, coarse files which the rebels carried in their sheaths, and gashes disfigured heads and faces." 19

The Bowie knife was the unofficial knife during the conflict, and many makers, especially Sheffield makers, got into the spirit of things by etching sediments on the blades of their Bowies. One Sheffield knife, made by W and H Whitehead about 1860 has, "Deathe to Trators" etched on the 8-inch blade to express Union sediments. One knife picked up off the battlefield of Southern Mountain is 11 inches in length with a seven-inch blade, the etching reads, 'The Land of the Free - The Home of the Brave.' The maker is Manson, of Sheffield. In an old newspaper, the *Slaves Friend*, Published by the American Anti-Slavery Society, at the price of one cent, there is a picture of a bowie Knife with, "Death to Abolition" etched in the blade. The title of the piece is *Bowie Knives*, and the writer says, "These horrid weapons are usually called bowie knives, they were invented by a man who lived in the state of Louisiana. His name was Buie. It is a French name, and is pronounced Boo-e. Afterwards he went to Texas and was killed there in battle.

"People in slave states often carry such knives about them. When they get angry they draw the knife, and sometimes stab one another!

"A man who keeps a shop in Broadway, New York city, sells Bowie knives. Several people in New York sell them. I saw one at his window. It had two words on the blade, etched in, as they call it. Perhaps you have seen razors with mottoes on the blade, in the same style. Do you want to know what two words were on the blade? I will tell you - "Death to Abolition." I asked the man a great many questions about these knives. He said, 'the knives were imported from England by several merchants in this city. He told me the names of two of them. One keeps his store in Pearl Street, and the other in Maiden Lane.'

"The man said also that bowie knives are made at Newark, New Jersey, and Springfield, Massachusetts, but he never saw any with the words, "death to abolition" on them, except those imported from England. But one seller said he could have the words put on

Vannoy

here if purchasers wished it. How wicked to make such knives! How wicked to sell them!! How wicked to use them!!!" 20

Although many soldiers carried fighting knives, they were not the only knives during the war. Pocket or jackknives were usually in the soldiers' possession, and a table knife of some sort was often seen, although sheath knives would work in a pinch for cutting meat or bread.

One interesting knife that was used during the war was the patented knife, fork and spoon combination, that folded into a Barlow-like handle, and was easily carried as a pocket-knife. One of these was found bearing the name, Richard's Patent, July 23, 1861, and was carried by a Georgia soldier. It is about eight inches long, and consists of a knife, fork and spoon that lock together. Many soldiers found these to be durable, and easier to keep track of than the separate cutlery that was often provided. These were sold by firms such as Nathan Ames, Saugus Center, Mass, patented, 1861, WM H Richards, Newton, Mass, patent, 1861,(perhaps the Richard mentioned above.), and J.P. Snow and Co., Hartford, Connecticut and Chicago.

In an account from the Civil War, by a Carlton McCarthy, gives us a look at the Confederate soldier, outfitted and ready for battle. "On his back he strapped a knapsack containing a full stock of underwear, soap, towels, comb, brush, looking-glass, tooth-brush, paper and envelopes, pens, ink, pencils, blacking, photographs, smoking and chewing tobacco, pipes, twine string, and cotton strips for wounds and other emergencies, needles and thread, buttons, knife, fork and spoon, and many other things as each man's idea of what he was to encounter varied." 21

The bayonet saw much use in the Civil War, as it did in the Revolutionary War earlier. The bayonet is an ancient weapon, making a gun into a long knife, and very effective on the flintlocks, that took time to reload. Many references are made to bayonets and bayonet wounds during the Civil War.

Although not really knives, many bayonets used by the Confederate troops were simply large bowie knives with rings welded on so they could be slipped over the gun barrel, and removed when the soldier needed a knife. Carlton McCarthy, describing the soldiers' life in the Army of Northern Virginia, wrote, "The infantry found out

Sharp Edges

that bayonets were not of much use, and did not hesitate to throw them, with the scabbard, away." Colonel Fremantle observed of the Arkansas brigade: "Most of them were armed with Enfield rifles captured from the enemy. Many, however, had lost or thrown away their bayonets, which they don't appear to value properly, as they assert that they have never met any Yankees who would wait for that weapon." 22

However, with the many references to bayonet fighting, very few must have thrown them away. In the battle at Sportsylvania, called The Bloody Angle, fought May 12, 1864, and observer wrote: "Skulls were crushed with clubbed muskets, and men stabbed to death with swords and bayonets thrust between the logs in the parapet which separated the combatants." 23 Private W.H. Cummingham of the 19th Alabama wrote of the fighting at Chickamauga: "The days work was one continual charge of the bayonet - that terrible weapon which invariably wins when properly manned and used in the right cause." 24

During the siege of Petersburg, VA, John Wise, student at Virginia Military Institute, wrote of the battle the soldiers advanced within a few feet of the enemy, and "with their guns almost upon the bodies of their foes, delivered deadly fire, and, rushing upon them with bayonets and clubbed muskets, drove them pell-mell back into the entrenchment which they had just left." 25

One incident occurred during the battle of Chickamauga, where General Preston who, "....coolly examines each man's cartridge-box and says, "Men, we must use the bayonet, - the bayonet, - we will give them the bayonet!" 26

One writer, Charles Johnson, who was assigned hospital duty, wrote that he had never seen a wound made by a bayonet thrust, and only one made by a sword. Either the edged weapons were thrust hard enough to kill in most cases, or were slight enough not to merit medical attention.

Most of the suppliers who made swords and knives also made bayonets, such as Ames, Brown and Tetley, to name a few.

Although we don't think of the Civil War as being fought on the high seas, the Navy did see action at various times during the conflict. Sailors carried clasp knives for cutting and splicing ropes and other odd jobs that required a sharp blade. They also helped to

Vannoy
pass the long hours aboard ship by whittling and carving. If a sailor became tangled in a running line, a knife could mean the difference between life and death, clasp knives were issued to sailors during the War. The first identifiable clasp knife issued was a jackknife with a single blade, about three inches long, with a rounded almost beak point. The handle was antler, the bolster forged iron. It was stamped, US Navy, obviously used by the Federal Navy. It seems these knives were made in Sheffield and supplied through an American jobber.

In the book, Confederate Arms, Albaugh and Simmons write; "As a weapon for foot artillery, the short sword was a poor thing, but the Naval short sword was a different matter. This was a most deadly weapon in the days of boarding and wooden ships." 27 These were smaller than swords, but not as small a belt knife, however, many bowies were long enough to be classed as short swords. The Naval short sword was a double-edged weapon, and could be used as an ax as much as a sword. A number of these were made by Thomas, Griswold & Co., New Orleans.

In one reference, made by a Confederate privateer, from the ship, Ivy, that later was taken into the Confederate navy. Privateers did considerable damage to Union shipping during the first year of the war. In a letter by M. Repard, he writes: "We lie in or near the river every night, but start out soon after midnight, and keep a sharp lookout for any speck on the horizon, and when the cry of "sail-ho!" is heard the Ivy's "tendrils" don revolvers, swords, knives and rifles with great excitement and good nature." 28

Although carried into the war as weapons or utility tools, knives, as everywhere, often saw a variety of uses, such as during the battle of the Wilderness, as told by Private Walter Gross, who fought with the 2nd Massachusetts. "Here we began to construct rifle-pits, by piling up logs and throwing up the soil against them. For this purpose men used their tin-drinking-cups, bayonets, and case-knives....." 29

Field hospitals put knives to use nearly everyday, and in one eyewitness account, writer Carl Schurz, famous politician and reformer who commanded the XI Corps at Gettysburg, writes in his "The Reminiscences of Carl Schurz; "There stood the surgeons, their sleeves rolled up to the elbows, their bare arms as well as their linen aprons smeared with blood, their knives not seldom held between

Sharp Edges

their teeth, while they were helping a patient on or off the table, or had their hands otherwise occupied; around them pools of blood and amputated arms or legs in heaps, sometimes more than man-high. Antiseptic methods were still unknown at that time. As a wounded man was lifted on the table, often shrieking with pain as the attendants handled him, the surgeon quickly examined the wound and resolved upon cutting off the injured limb. Some ether was administered and the body put in position in a moment. The surgeon snatched his knife from between his teeth, where it had been while his hands were busy, wiped it rapidly once or twice across his blood-stained apron, and the cutting began." 30

    A report in the Charleston Mercury, July 20, 1864, tells of the wounded who, "will linger for a time under the knife and saw of the surgeons and then perhaps return to their homes maimed for life." 31

    Knives as weapons were not limited to the battlefield. In April 1860, tempers were running high in the house and senate. Fist fights were common, and in one instance, in the House, a group of Southerners led by Roger A. Pryor of Virginia, tried to silence Owen Lovejoy of Illinois during one of his denunciations of slavery. John Fox Potter, Wisconsin, the official records say, yelled, "This side shall be heard, let the consequences be what they may." Pryor accused Potter of composing the statement and inserting it into record after the event. Heated words followed, and Pryor's seconds waited on Potter.

    Potter, it is said, issued a challenge to Pryor. He said he would be glad to oblige the Virginian in a duel, in a closed room with bowie knives of equal weight and length of blade. The fight, he said, would continue until one participant fell, adding that he "would endeavor to carve him, (Pryor) so skillfully as forever to remove his desire to fight." Potter didn't have to, the challenge was enough to remove any desire for a fight. Newspapers grabbed at the story, and knives were sent to him from all parts of the nation, including one from the Republicans of the State of Missouri, a seven-foot knife bearing the inscription, "I will always keep a Prior engagement." and the name, "Bowie Knife Potter" clung to him for the rest of his life. 31

    When President Lincoln was assassinated it is said that Booth, " He held a knife in one hand and a pistol in the other."

    Also, on the same night that Lincoln was killed, an

Vannoy
accomplice of Booth's, Lewis Paine, made an unsuccessful attempt at the life of Secretary of State Seward, this time with a Sheffield made Bowie knife with an alligator embossed on the German silver handle.

In an old newspaper account, on April 16, 1865, we find that Mr. Seward will recover from his wound.

The Civil War has captured the imagination of writers and scholars for over 100 years, it was fought on American soil, and pitted Americans against themselves. It cut the country in half, and sediments on both sides ran high.

The war changed the face of America, and changed the face of war-fare. It was the first modern war, where railroads, trenches and mines became a part of warfare, and where new inventions, such as telegraph lines, photography, and balloon observation came into use. It was one of the last wars where men still fought hand to hand, instead of picking off targets from a distance. The popularity of the bayonet, the bowie, and the saber as weapons declined, leaving room for the Spencer and the Henry rifle, and more effective, if less romantic, instruments of war.

Sharp Edges

Chapter 9

Knives of the Army on The Western Frontier

1866-1886

Throughout history, the mounted forces have been an important part of the armed forces, but never has the Cavalry in the U.S. been as important as they were during the Indian wars, that covered mainly the 20 years between 1866 and 1886, when troops were needed to protect emigrants, gold seekers, and settlers from Indian attacks.

Many cavalrymen came direct from the Civil War to enlist for service on the plains. The great distances, and pursuit of a more skilled and better-mounted foe, made the cavalry a necessity. Practically everyone in the west was mounted, to steal a horse was a crime second to murder, and the army was no exception. Foot soldiers were practically useless, so the plains army was, by necessity, a mounted unit, although there were units of infantry as well.

In the book, Military Life in Dakota, a journal by Philippe Regis de Trobriand, who had been a colonel in the Army of the United States, veteran of the Civil War, and commander of a post in Dakota in 1867, writes, "From these facts it follows, 1. That the infantry is absolutely useless in pursuing Indians on the "warpath", and must be left in garrisons." And, "That the cavalry is the only arm that can be used effectively in pursuing Indians." 1

Called "Yellow-legs" by the Indians for the yellow strip down

Vannoy

the leg of the blue trousers, these men had a hard life. Forts were drafty, barely heated places during the cold, harsh winters, and hot, windy hellholes in the summers. "The mercury rises to +110 degrees F. in the shade during the day....there are terrible windstorms from time to time. Last week the whole camp just missed being blown into the river.....a sheet iron stove was rolled up to the foot of the plateau by the storm." 2

Winters were even worse. George App, part of the Third Infantry campaigning in the Northern Rocky Mountains wrote: ....a blizzard suddenly set in and they were snow bound for five days. They had tents for shelter, but the cold was intense, and there was a careful check each morning to see if any succumbed to the cold over night. Several of the soldiers died in their sleep and were found frozen stiff in the morning." 3

Wages were low, from 13.00 to $16.00 per month for a private, somewhat higher for an officer.

Even before the end of the Civil War, the Indians on the Western Plains, feeling the push of white settlers, began to push back angrily. Union troops and volunteers were sent to keep the Indians at bay. By the end of the Civil War, the plains were a battleground, the Regular Army was sent West to battle the redman. On July 28, 1866, four new cavalry regiments, the 7th through the 10th, were to be stationed throughout the West to restore order on the frontier as well as additional artillery and infantry regiments. In 1866, around 54,302 men were listed as army personnel.

Between the time Lewis and Clark scouted the land west of the Mississippi River and end of the Civil War, men believe that the Great Plains, or the "Great American Desert" was unfit for white men, or settlers. They preferred to cross it to get to the richer lands of Oregon, Washington, or golden California. "Let the Indians and Buffalo have it" was the general feeling. So treaties were written leaving much of the land to the tribes. The cry of gold changed much of this, Gold in California, Gold in the sacred Black Hills, Gold in Montana. Gold Fever. Men moved into the desert, found it livable, and wanted to stay. But the Indians had to be removed. The army had it's hands full, on one hand, trying to maintain the peace among the Indians, who saw that white men didn't honor the treaties, and protect the white men who, actually, didn't have any

Sharp Edges

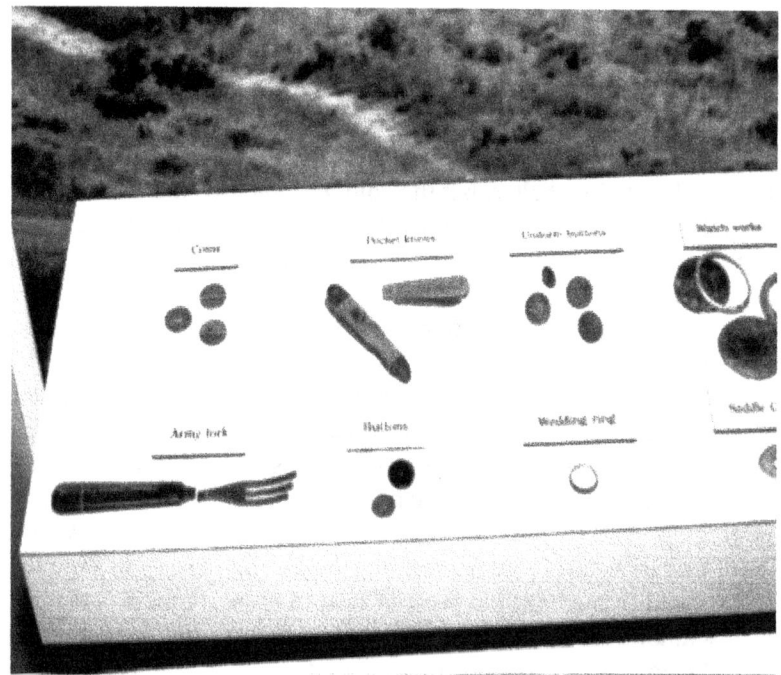

Some artifacts, including two pocketknives, found on the Little Big Horn Battlefield site. (Photo by author, knives courtesy of the Custer Battlefield Museum, Garryowen, Montana.)

business being in Indian lands. There were hostilities to be put down on both sides, and the Cavalry was often caught in the middle.

Campaigning on the plains was lonely business, and a trooper had to have faith in his comrades, his horse, his gun and his knife. Although references are scare, and the army didn't issue knives to the plains troops until 1880, nearly every soldier had a knife, usually two, a jackknife and a sheath knife. Harold Petersen, in American Knives writes: "Any man who has been in a combat area knows how highly a soldier prizes his knife....especially in the lengths to which he will go to obtain one that meets his personal requirements..... Then nothing would stand in their way until they got it. Money, food, trophies, anything - even whiskey, would be offered until the sale was made." 4

Nearly every make and style of knife that was available at the time might have found it's self on an army post. Green River knives, bowies carried during the Civil War, Sheffield knives, jack knives and pocketknives have all been found at old army sites, or passed down in families.

Most references, when they mention knives at all, mention butchers, skinners, hunting knives or Bowies. But whatever the style or make, knives were as important to the soldier on the plains as they were to soldiers in the Civil War, or to soldiers in World War I.

It is rather amazing why, when the men were in such a primitive environment as the plains, that the U.S. Government didn't issue knives to the troops, except in 1848, when, "Company E was alone in being issued the sole regulation edged weapon for the Mounted Rifles. This was the Model 1849 Rifleman's Knife. In 1848 the U.S. Ordnance Department had purchased 1,000 of these weapons from the Ames Manufacturing Company of Cabotville, Massachusetts. The double-edged, spear point blade was just under a foot in length and was carried in a handsome brass-tipped black leather scabbard. There are no authenticated accounts of the Ames knife being used in combat, but it doubtless made a handy camp tool." 5

According to Firearms Traps and Tools of the Mountain Men, the price was $4.00 per knife, a hefty sum in 1848. The hilt was walnut, and the guard brass. Russell says, "It is a doughy piece, longer and heavier than the Army knives that preceded it in the 1830's - the Hicks knife and its variants." 6

Sharp Edges

It was not until 1880, when the Springfield Armory manufactured the model 1880 hunting knife, which carried the mark, "U.S./ SPRINGFIELD", that the government actually issued knives to the troops on the Indian campaigns.

Why they waited until 1880, when the Indian campaigns were nearly ended to issue a knife is unusual. But the 1880 knife was designed for use on the frontier, with three purposes in mind: It was to be a butcher knife for beef and wild game; it was to be an entrenching tool; and a last ditch weapon. These knives have an 8 1/2 inch blade, two inches wide, single edged with a spear point. A leather scabbard was made for the knife and included with it.

In the book, Forty Miles a Day on Beans and Hay, I did find one reference, I believe, to these Springfield knives. It is the correct time frame, it was after the turmoil subsided on the Sioux reservations early in 1891, when the men of the Eighth Infantry marched into Chadron, Nebraska to reach the railhead. "The peaceful population that night took to the hills or barricaded their homes, and the boys proceeded to decorate the town a bright red......(During the night an eighteen inch snow fell, covering the packs and other equipment the soldiers had hastily left by the railroad tracks.) There was enough equipment left under the snow to equip a company of militia. I myself lost a cartridge belt and a trench knife." (wrote August Hettinger) 7

As the reference says, trench knife, rather than bowie or hunting knife, it is undoubtedly the Springfield knife.

Even before 1880, the soldiers used knives on campaigns and around the post.

Knives were not used as much for defense, except for some cases of last-ditch weapons, as they were as essential tools on the frontier. Food was often bad, hardtack, salt pork, beans, coffee, and coarse bread. For variety, many times the officers sent the men out hunting for wild game to relieve their diets, and knives were of the essence when it came to skinning and gutting game.

Some officers, such as General George A. Custer and others, were great hunters, in fact, Custer felt that hunting buffalo from horseback with a pistol was good training for his men, and hunters carried knives. In 1876, just before the Battle of the Little Big Horn, Custer is described as wearing campaign dress, with, "A Remington

Vannoy

Sporting Rifle....two bulldog self-cocking English white handled pistols...a hunting knife in a beaded fringed scabbard." 8

In General Orders No. 77, issued by General Reynolds, headquarters Department of Texas there are two references to knives as they are used in campaigns. "The inspector will see that such soldier, (before he leaves for field service) is provided with arms and equipments.......That he has the prescribed amount of ammunition; good shoes, a change of underclothing; haversack, canteen, knife, fork, spoon, tin cup tin plate....." And, later in the Orders, "When it is determined upon before night that such a camp is to be made, the men with their knives, (if there be no scythes along) should cut grass enough for the horses and mules for the night." 9 This was in case of making a camp in Indian country when danger of an attack is impending. As with most mounted units during war, the horse was cared for first, as without a mount a soldier was, really, at mercy of not only Indians by nature as well.

On one campaign, General Crook was chasing a band of Indians, and, to increase the speed, he left the supply wagons behind. They chased the Sioux for 11 days, and the supplies began to run low, and the exhausted horses began dropping to the ground as if shot. The starving troopers fell to butchering and eating the horses, and one man remarked, "It seemed like cannibalism." 10

Knives were used as all around tools, and many times knives were depended upon to keep the soldiers' rifles and Colt pistols in operation. The Colt .45 pistol was a great improvement over the older arms, but occasionally it would give problems to the man using it. As it reads in book, Bugles, Banners, and Warbonnets, "Screws in the Colt were seldom tightened, and only after lengthy firings was this necessary." If these grew too loose, the ejector-tube housing was slow in ejecting spent cartridges. "To correct this, the trooper had to keep a screwdriver on hand or use the point of his knife to tighten the screw." 11

The Springfield Model 70 rifle, Government Issue, also had a few problems that the men cussed and discussed. One of these was that the ejector spring would cut through the head of the cartridge, leaving it in the gun after the rest of the shell had been ejected. This left the soldier powerless until he picked out the empty shell with the point of a knife, if he was lucky enough to have one." 12

Sharp Edges

Curley, the crow scout with Custer, said that he saw soldiers under fire using their hunting knives to unstick the cartridges in their rifles. "The soldiers were armed with single-shot 45-70 caliber Springfield carbines, and accurate and deadly weapon up to 600 yards. But when fired rapidly the breech became foul and the greasy cartridges often jammed and could not be removed by the extractor. This meant that the empty shell had to be forced out by the blade of a hunting knife," said Sergeant Charles Windolph in his book, "I Fought with Custer." 13.

"Some historians have felt that the rifles jamming was the cause of the Custer defeat," Doerner said. "But Custer was just out-manned and out-gunned by the Native American forces. He couldn't have won." As in much of history, there are many conflicting reports on the battle. One of these conflicts is the fact that in movies and in artwork, and probably in fiction books, the cavalry is portrayed as riding with and fighting with cavalry sabers.

"The Hollywood version of Custer - pistol in one hand, saber in the other - is basically fiction," says John A. Doerner, Battlefield historian. "It's a glamorous perspective but far from the truth. The sabers were boxed up at the Powder River supply depot before they rode into the Little Big Horn Country."

Doerner added that the cavalry seldom would get within saber distance of the Indians in most battles, but said, "If Reno's command would have had sabers, they would have been close enough to use them."

The cavalry did have sabers, most were civil war leftovers, but they didn't always carry them on campaigns on the plains. "When the army of the plains received a 'light marching order' they had to move fast and with stealth, much like the Indians. The sabers in their nickel scabbards clanked. The sound of the cavalry on the move was a constant clanking of saber against metal or saddle leather. The cavalry made a lot of noise, tin cups and utensils and sabers," Doerner said. "The scabbards were made of shiny nickel, and the sun would glint off the scabbards, betraying the position of the cavalry. Many soldiers painted the scabbards to cut the glare."

Doerner said that sabers were used on the plains, but not specifically for combat. "Once the cavalry was on campaign in North Dakota," he told me at the Battlefield. "One big problem was

Vannoy

rattlesnakes in the camp, so they used the sabers to clear away the snakes." What would John Wayne have done?

Although most of the sabers were packed away, two officers, 1st Lt. Edward Mathey Gustave and Lt. Charles DeRudio, chose to retain their sabers for the campaign. de Rudio was with Reno at the Valley fight, and Gustave was with Captain Benteen and later joined Reno's command. The sabers were not used in either battle, they were either packed away or still on the horses, Doerner's historic sources said.

But, if the cavalry didn't use sabers, at least in one recorded instance, the Indians did. In an interview with Eagle Elk, of the Ogalala Sioux, in the book, Lakota Recollections of the Custer Fight, he said, "There were two Indians....chasing the soldiers. Suddenly, the man on the white horse got among the soldiers. He had a sword and used it to kill one soldier." 14

While swords are more romantic and ingrained into the fictional psyche, knives, although seldom mentioned, were used everywhere on the plains, including at the battle.

After the battle of the Little Big Horn, in a letter to General S.V. Benet, M.A. Reno wrote, "An Indian scout who was with that portion of the Regt. which Custer took into battle, relating what he saw in that part of the battle, says that from his hiding place he could see the men sitting down under fire and working at their guns, a story that finds confirmation in the fact that the officers, who afterwards examined the battlefield, as they were burying the dead, found knives with broken blades laying near the dead bodies." 15 This statement has come under fire in recent years, but the author will stand by it, as it was the way those near the battle saw it. Some writers have said that the knives were Indian knives, left after the battle, but a diarist near the battle wrote that the Indians seldom left knives, considering them to valuable.

"Indians had skinning knives, scalping knives, and trade knives," Doerner said. "The soldiers had personal pocket knives and hunting knives. Knives were used to skin and dress game, for survival should a soldiers be separated from the main body of the troop, for cutting meat at the table, and for general camp use. An army scout would use theirs for close combat. A knife would have been indispensable to a good solider or warrior."

Sharp Edges

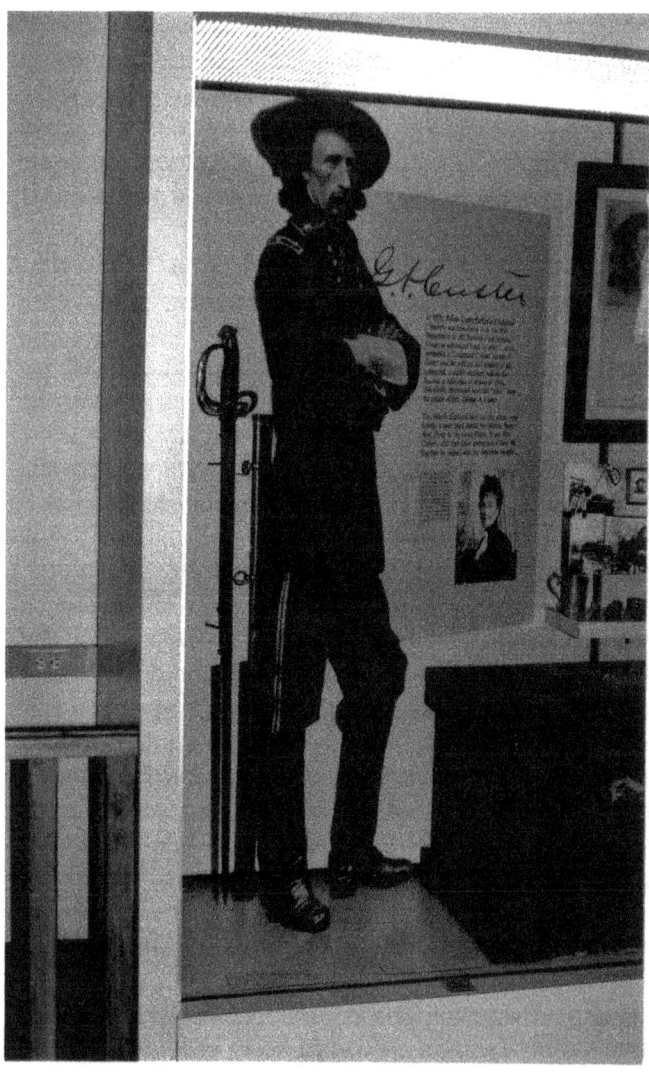

General Custer and his sword. Photo by author, sword courtesy of Little Big Horn Battlefield National Mounment Museum

Vannoy

"Knives came in handy to make entrenchments and rifle pits as well," Doerner added. In the book, I Fought With Custer, Sergeant Windolph says, "...We had been busy too, digging shallow holes with our mess kits, our steel knives and forks and with our fingers." 16. Windolph was with Troop H, under Benteen, and was stationed to the south of massacre hill, along the Little Big Horn River.

Knives have been found on the battlefield during current archeology digs, but many were lost. Indians may have carried many off right after the battle, and souvenir seekers collected them in later years.

One knife found at the battlefield was a 5-cent pocket- knife "These cheap, small, handy knives were popular with soldiers and civilians alike," Doerner said. Many of the pocket- knives found were little different from the knives we can buy over any discount store counter today, and were remarkably well preserved.

The Indians carried mainly hunting type or butcher type knives. Crazy Horse was known to have always carried a hunting knife.

At the Agate Bluffs Beds Museum near Crawford, Nebraska, there is a sheath with whetstone in it that Crazy Horse carried to keep his knife razor sharp.

Many knives were stolen from whites and dead soldiers, and many were received as trade goods. By the time of the Little Big Horn Battle, the Indians had been using white man's steel bladed knives for nearly a century for hunting, scalping and general survival.

In an interview with Red Feather, an Ogalala Lakota in 1991 he talked about the Little Big Horn battle. Red Feather and Kicking Bear encountered two Indian scouts from the Custer troops. They shot one and caught the other, "Red Feather stabbed him to death," he reports in the interview. 14.

Indians were masters at making do with what they had, and captured knives and gunstocks from dead soldiers could be made into a formidable weapon by inserting the knife blade into the rifle stock, making a sharp edged club. "...the Indians (were) using war clubs as the principal weapon," 15.

In one incident, the Indians followed soldiers trying to escape on foot and "...killed them with war clubs of stone and wooden

Sharp Edges

clubs, some of the latter having lance spears on them." 16. The Indians, according to the narrative by Iron Hawk, knocked the soldiers from their horses and killed them with war clubs. Iron Hawk was a Hunkpapa Lakota who was born in Montana in 1862, who fought against Custer at the Little Big Horn.

Tomahawks, an edged weapon similar to a hatchet, were also used by the Native American troops in the Custer fight. In an interview recorded in *Lakota Recollections,* with Moving Robe Woman, she says, "In the charge, the Indians rode among the troopers and with tomahawks unhorsed several of them." 17.

During the plains wars, the Indians used knives for a more gruesome purpose. Scalping had been an accepted part of Indian warfare since the Spanish introduced the custom in the 1600s, but many tribes took the mutilation of the enemy even further.

"The Indians did not scalp any of Custer's men; but they did scalp all of Reno's men who were killed," 8 relates Nicholas Ruleau, in *Lakota Recollections.* He was a man of French extraction who acted as an interpreter and talked to many Indians after the Custer fight. He lived on the Pine Ridge Reservation since 1879.

One reason given for not scalping the soldiers was related by Hollow Horn Bear of the Brule Lakota tribe in an interview in the book in 1909. "Why were so few of the soldiers scalped at point "G"? the interviewer asked.

"Hair was too short," Hollow Horn Bear said.

Doerner, at the Battlefield Museum, added this, "Some tribes believed that if a body was missing a limb, the spirit could not make it into the after world, or some felt that if a body was disabled in this life they would be in the next life as well. Some felt that by cutting off the trigger finger of the dead enemy, they could not fight with the Indians in the afterlife."

Doerner added that Custer's trigger finger was severed by the Sioux, and that there was a trigger-finger necklace at the Buffalo Bill Cody Museum in Cody, Wyoming.

White men, to, such as Chivington at Sand Creek, used knives to mutilate the bodies of the Indians, some women and children.

But, mostly, knives were tools, used for utility work, such as picking stones out of horses' hooves, (most carried a jack-knife as

Vannoy

well as a belt knife, and some may have had hoof-picks as well as knife blades.)

Diaries of the times also mention knives being used for cutting sod for graves, such as after the battle of the Little Big Horn, and to dig rifle pits, such as in 1868, when Major George Forsysth and his force used tin plates and hunting knives to dig rifle pits when they were surrounded by a large force of Indians.

Undoubtedly, knives were also used for removing bullets and arrowheads when the surgeons were not present, from both horses and men. As Texas Ranger "Put" Putney said in a recorded interview, "I've dug more bullets out of horse than I have out of men." 21. On a campaign in the Wilderness, cavalry officers would have to do the same thing.

But, no matter where a knife came from, either from the fort blacksmith, whom I am sure made several knives for the soldiers, from Sheffield, or later, from the Springfield armory, knives played an important role in the campaigns of the Western plains, where the Yellow-Legs, or Long Knives, (referring to sabers) were sent out to protect the white adventurers from the "savages" who were only protecting what they had held sacred for so many generations.

Sharp Edges

Chapter 10
Knives of the Trail Hands

Following the civil war, when herds of wild eyed Texas cattle had to be smoked out of the their homes in the mesquite thickets, and Eastern markets were crying for beef, a new culture was being born west of the Mississippi River. Men came west, hoping for adventure, and the wide-open spaces. Many of these men came into Texas, or came back to Texas, many smarting from the defeat of the south, and looking for some kind of living.

The many of the Texas longhorns had been left when the owners went to war, and bred prolifically, and learned to live like wild animals rather than barnyard pets. Most were unbranded, and became property of the man with the longest loop.

Enterprising ranchers hired young, strong men for a $1 a day and found to collect the cattle, brand them, and, during the 1870's, convince them to trail in herds of well over a thousand towards the railheads, and from there to the eastern markets. A new culture, with a mix of American youths, Negro hands, and a strong sprinkling of Mexican and Spanish influence from the southern states, a new, romantic figure emerged. The saddle of the cowboys, with the long stirrups, the horn for dallying the rope around, the high swells and high cantle to help the man ride the rough broncos that were a part of the work, came almost directly from Mexico, with little variation. The lariat or la reata as well is of Spanish origin, and the broad-brimmed hat a scaled down version of the sombrero. The American's contributed the Winchester, the Colt, and the Bowie Knife: The trail herds and the chuck wagon.

The cowboy, still thrills the imagination some 100 years later. Tough, wild, reckless, at home only in the saddle, or in a bedroll under the stars, these romantic figures became legends.   Riding,

Vannoy

roping, shooting, became their legacy, but they also carried knives. Knives have practically been forgotten.

When one thinks of the cowboy, one thinks of his trusty Colt Peacemaker and the Winchester 30-30 rifle. But knives were important, probably more important even than the cowboys' firearms.

Like other periods of history, the knife was such a common tool as to be largely ignored by writers of the times. Occasionally references are made, but they are generic in content.

As most of the cowboys came west fresh from the Civil War, the knife that was most common on the new frontier during the early days was the bowie. As with knife makers today, the term bowie covers a wide variety of knife styles, and came to mean basically any large, clip-pointed knife with a metal guard. Cowboys used bowie knives for a variety of tasks, carrying them in a leather scabbard, usually on the left side so as not to interfere with their pistol, or on the right side behind their pistol.

Charles Siringo, cowboy author, wrote of Shanghai Pearce, the biggest cattleman in the West, with 100,000 longhorns. Pearce writes: I have often seen Pearce honing his big knife on his bootleg.

The blade was about fourteen inches long, double-edged, and tapering to a point. The knife could cut a reata dangling in the air. It was a throwing knife. Pearce showed me the proper manner in which to test a throwing blade. He rested the back of the blade on the forefinger at a certain point according to the total length of the weapon. You see, the smith who makes such a blade distributes the weight of his steel according to the throwing range. Pearce's knife was machined to turn twice in a throwing range of thirty feet." [1]

The southwest developed even more of a knife culture, as knives have been a part of the Spanish-American culture since the conquistadors. A cowboy of Mexican or Spanish ancestry was seldom without his knife, and it was a point of honor and courage to face your enemy with a knife in hand to hand combat, much as the English favored the "gentlemen's" art of pistol dueling. In old California, where the Spanish cowboy culture flourished before the gold rush, knives were often used. "After the roundup, at the mass cattle slaughters known as matanzas, he (the Spanish cowboy) would ride down upon one steer after another, killing each beast with a single flashing thrust of the long knife carried in his boot

Sharp Edges

An old photo of Charles Augustus Johnson, Company E, Frontier Battalion. It was made circa 1892. Note the large knife on his belt. Courtesy of the "Texas State Library and Archives Commission." (Prints & Photographs # 1/32-1.)

scabbard." 2 These long knives were probably a variation of the Spanish Dagger, or dirk, which was also the forerunner of the famous American Bowie knife.

Although usually used as tools, occasionally, though, cowboys did get into fights with their knives, usually Bowies, or Arkansas Toothpicks, a long, pointed dagger beveled on both sides. In the book, The West That Was, John Leakey tells of a fight in a saloon in Dickinson, ND. The fight started when a young Norwegian lost his money in a poker game, where Massy, Leakey's acquaintances, had done some winning in. The Norweign called Massey back into the wine room, and called John's name. "When I went in he had Massy by the collar and was holding an old deer-foot butcher knife against his throat.

"You give me twenty dollars or I cut his throat. he told me.

"I don't have twenty dollars." I said

"Then I asked Massy, "Do you want me to give him twenty dollars?"

"I guess I'll have to," Massy said, looking cross-eyed at the knife under his nose.

"Why don't you let him go get the money for you?" I asked the Norwegian.

"He decided he would, but he still held onto Massy's collar with one hand and the knife with the other."

As they neared the bar, the Norwegian grabbed a six-shooter, and, as he did so, let loose of Massy's collar. They had a scuffle, and when the Norwegian broke loose and ran, John Leakey grabbed him and Massy knocked him out with a well-placed gun butt.

Leakey said after the incident. "I was twenty-three years old then, and six feet, six inches tall. For quite a while I'd figured I was pretty well able to take care of myself - but that little affair was a lesson to me." 3

In fiction, knives received even more attention as weapons. In Monte Walsh, one of Jack Schaffer's best works, Monte gets into it with a Mexican over a woman, "Out of the corner of vision, from the left, he saw the one man rushing, knife in hand,...." Monte grabs the man's wrist, knees him in the groin, and, "in the instant of action he was aware of the other man, from the right and behind now, and he felt the tearing shock of the other knife slicing in and grating on a rib

Sharp Edges

...." 5 Monte is laid up for a few days, but is soon back on his feet.

In Ride the Dark Trail, by Louie L'Amour, Logan Sackett, the main character, confronts Mexican Joe Herrara in a comical scene. "Herrara never took his eyes off me. He was mean, I knew that, and he'd cut up several men with his knife. He had a way of taking it out and honing it until sharp, then with a yell he'd jump you and start cutting." Mexican Joe " got out his whetstone, but before he could draw his knife I drew mine. "Say, just what I need." Before he knew what I was going to do I had reached over and taken the stone. Then I began whetting my own blade." Logan sharpens his knife, tests the edge, and passes the stone back to Joe. "Gracias," I said, smiling friendly-like. "A man never knows when he'll need a good edge."

Sackett goes on to describe his knife, "My knife was a sort of modified Bowie, but made by the Tinker. No better knives were ever made than those made by the Tinker back in Tennessee."

"I showed them the knife. "That there," I said, "is a Tinker-made knife. It will cut through most blades and will cut a man shoulder to belt with one stroke." 6

Several ranches during the 1870s, the most famous being the XIT ranch in western Texas, had written rules and regulations governing their cowhands, and often these included a ruling against using, "dirks, daggers, and bowies in the act of knife fighting."

Although seldom mentioned by name, or makers name, references crop up to knives in various writings of the period, such as in the book, Old Time Cowhand by Ramon Adams. He writes that during an electrical storm on the plains, where lightening created a serious hazard to anything that was above ground level, and the cowboy atop a horse made a conspicuous target, cowhands hurriedly got shut of six guns, spurs, knives, anything made of metal. Often this also included saddles with silver concos and metal stirrup bands, and bridles with metal bits, leaving the cowboy to fashion a halter out of his reata.

A knife was used for everything. Dressing out a deer or a steer for the cook pot, (chuck wagon cooks had several knives,) cutting the rope when one tied into a wild cow and the horse went down, cutting a wet cinch to lighten the load when in a bind in the water, opening tins of food, or cans of beer, cutting rawhide for ropes, digging bullets out of horses and men, digging the stone out of a

Vannoy

cowponies hoof on the trail; for playing mumblety-peg or whittling to kill time during the slow months of winter.

In Andy Adam's, Log of a Cowboy, one of the best books written about the old trail days, one use for a knife was to establish ownership of a cow. "In order to get at the brand, which was on the side, we turned the cow over, when Flood took out his knife and cut the hair away, leaving the brand easily traceable." 8

A cowboy found many uses for his sheath knife, and nearly as many for his pocketknife, which was usually carried as well as a sheath knife, and often referred to as a Barlow. The original Barlow knife was manufactured in the mid-17th century in England, legend has it that a man named Barlow designed the knife because he wanted to produce a rugged knife at the cheapest possible price. The blade was high carbon steel, with the bolster increased in length and weight. Usually, the bolster of a Barlow is about one-third the length of the closed knife. The handle was usually bone, with little finishing. No one has yet determined if the Barlow was actually produced by a man named Barlow, but it has been around a long time, with the first record in America being in 1779, and, according to Petersen, it seems to have been in general use at that time. American makers such as John Russell, who is credited as the first American cutler to manufacture the Barlow, manufactured several different knives.

With his version of the Barlow knife, Russell made the Russell name and Barlow name synonymous with the Russell Barlow knife, used by many cowboys, and often being the first coveted knife of a young boy, who wore it as a badge of his coming manhood, and gained immortality in the classics, Tom Sawyer and Huck Finn.

Pocketknives were most often seen during the brandings, when calves were earmarked with the owners particular distinguishing mark, be it a slit ear, cropped ear, under or over bite, or

The infamous "jingle-bob" ear mark of the John Chisum ranch in New Mexico, reported by one man to be the ugliest mutilation of a cow he had ever seen, and castrated, to live out their lives as grass loving steers.

In Cowboy Culture, by David Dray, and Adam's Old Time Cowhand, knives are mentioned as a part of the branding. Dray writes: "Another cowboy takes out his pocket knife-probably sharpened for the occasion-and begins to mark the calf's ear." 8

Sharp Edges

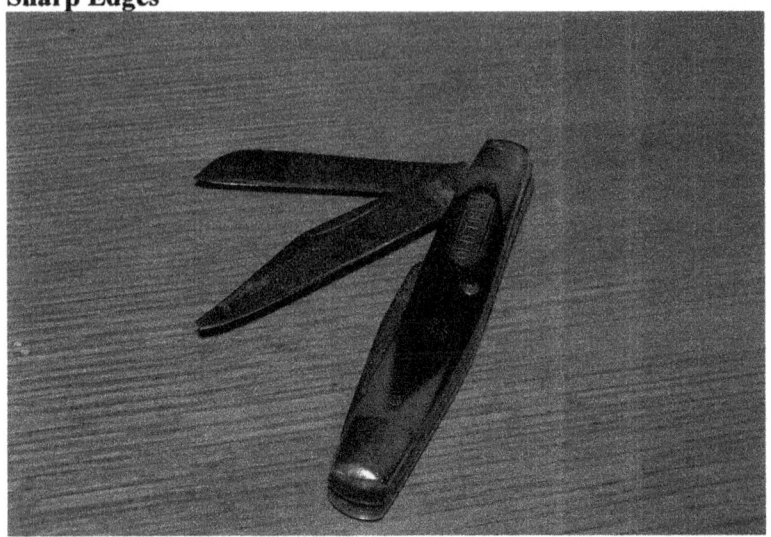

A three blade pocket knife, virtually unchanged since the trail drive days, and still a necessary part of the cowboy's regalia today. (Author's collection)

Vannoy

Adams calls these men "earmarkers," butchers, knifemen or cutters. "They squatted on their heels, building cigarettes, and sharpened their knives on little whetstones while the irons were gettin' hot. They used a cowman's ordinary knife which they resharpened every time the work slackened a bit. Not only did they mark the calves, but made future steers out of the young male animals." 9

The demand for pocket knives grew during the 1870's, and firms began making stockmen's or ranchers knives, selling them mainly to the Western market through the mail order catalogs. These were usually fairly large, with three blades, usually a spear point, a spey point blade, and a punch or a sheepsfoot blade, so the knife could be put to a variety of uses.

Ken Warner, in Knives '86, writes about modern stockmen's knives, but the quote could have been made in the 1870's just as well. "Take your cowboy, for example, and a lot of cowboys do keep a stock knife. Most quick cutting jobs are accomplished with the sheepsfoot blade, seems like. I feel that's because it's an easy blade to sharpen, and it humps up in the body enough to be easy to open, and it's a stout blade. The clip blade cleans game and fish and fingernails and does what slicing and point work there is. And the spey blade is often kept very, very keen and reserved for fine work like skinning, castration, and such." 10

Pocketknives even showed up in the cowboys songs, such as the song, Montana Horsewrangler, by Ed Sabers, which was sung often on the W Bar ranch in Montana, at the very end of the song, "Kiss your wife, put a heavy insurance on your life, And kill yourself with a pocket knife - I swear that's the best way." 11

Many times many a cowhand has probably felt the same way, although few followed through.

A knife was a constant companion, and a necessary tool for survival. A knife had to be strong, with good steel in the blade, because knives were as often ill-used as they were used. Opening tins, or cans, didn't do much for an edge, or prying or using the knife in place of a screwdriver or wire cutters.

In fact, I purchased an Old Timer pocketknife and on the box it informed the buyer that the knife was NOT a screwdriver or can opener. Not that it would stop any knife buyer from doing just that.

Sharp Edges

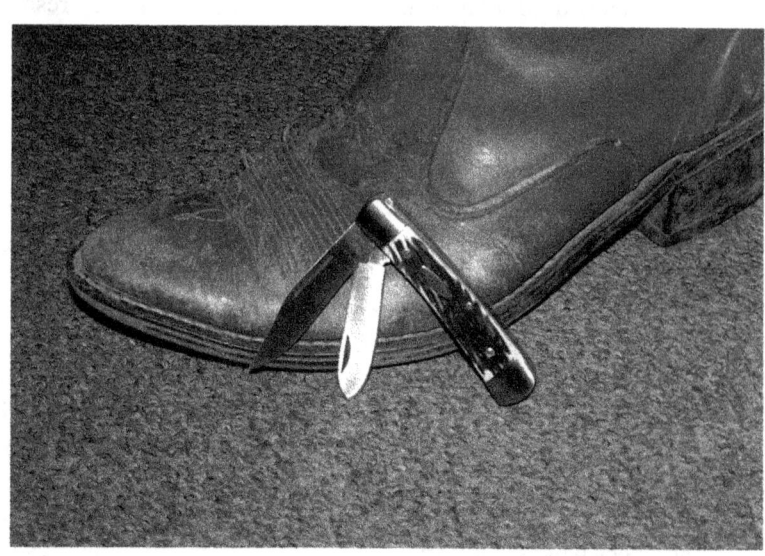

A modern Barlow-style two blade pocket knife such as a cowboy would have carried in the 1800's, and still carry today. (Author's collection)

Vannoy

Even today, nearly every rancher carries some sort of pocket knife, usually the three-bladed type, and the knife is still used much as it was in the Old West, for digging out stones from a horses foot, tightening screws, cutting baler twine, earmarking or castrating calves, or cutting slice of apple for a picnic. Knives are still playing their part in the West.

Chapter 11
Knives of the Frontier Gamblers

Gamblers were a colorful chapter in Western History, frequenting the saloons, the riverboats, and the trains, looking for honest or dishonest games, as long as there was a good chance of them winning.

Along with the gambler's lucky piece, and ever-present deck of cards, one of the most important parts of his dress was his weaponry, both knives and guns. Both were used for one purpose, to kill at close range, especially when a game got ugly, and the cry of "cheat" rang out across the green clothed table. Whether the gambler was actually cheating, or was simply a better card player than the rest of the players, he had to be ready to defend himself.

One of the common type knives used by gamblers on the frontier, was the push dagger, which originated in San Francisco. In The Book of Knives, in a caption on a photograph, reads, "Push daggers can be distinguished from each other by the shapes of their handles, but the principal remains the same for each - it is a weapon for concealment, and as such was favored by unscrupulous gamblers. The handle is gripped entirely by the hand, giving extreme force to the blow, which is often impossible to parry." 1 Push daggers had small handles, and short, dagger blades, usually not longer than 7 inches overall, with 4 inches being blade. In the book, American knives, by Petersen, there is a picture of a push dagger with the mark, "Wills & Finck/S.F. Cal." The dagger has a 4" blade with ivory grips. The iron scabbard is designed to hang upside down while the blade is retained by a spring.

Wills and Finck were cutlers often mentioned in San Francisco. From the book, Knifemakers of Old San Francisco, "Julius Finck sold gambling equipment, both crooked and square,

Vannoy

much of which he made himself. Finck's family might have made gambling and cheating equipment in Germany; their home town, Baden, was one of the gambling centers of nineteenth century Europe." 2 It is not exactly sure when he and Fred Will joined as partners, but they enjoyed a long and profitable partnership.

Wills and Finck were not the only ones manufacturing knives for the gambling trade. Michael Price, knife maker who came from Ireland in 1857, and set up a cutlery business Horance Bell, On the Old West Coast, written in 1908 and published in 1930 by William Morrow Co., said of Price, "He never made a knife for less than fifty dollars. A bowie knife, you know." 3 Many of these had gold, silver or mother-of-pearl handles, some were inlaid with diamonds. Price made several daggers and bowie knives, the most famous being one that San Francisco Judge David S. Terry, who was captured by the Vigilance Committee in 1856, and used his "....shining, ivory-hilted bowie knife.." to try and stab Deputy Marshal Farrish. (quoted from the San Francisco Examiner)

In the Time-Life Book, The Gamblers, it has a two-page spread of a gambler's weaponry, that is, knives. Like their clothes, gamblers often liked their knives flashy, and stylish, and many had the handles made of stag, abalone-shell, or fancy wood. Some even had inscriptions on the handle, like the one inscribed, "The Fifth Ace." as the book puts it, "The bowie knife at left is inscribed with its owners belief that it would win the pot if four aces in his hand proved insufficient." 4 Ben Thompson, one of the west's most violent gamblers, had a stag handle with his name on a silver insert.

About the weapons, the book says, "When a gamblers cheating-actual or imagined - was at issue, the weapons that sprang to hand were as macabre as they were deadly. From vests, sleeves, books, and wherever else ingenuity hid them came knuckle-duster knives, dirks, and push daggers. ..... The vogue for inconspicuous arms came west with gamblers who were migrating from notorious New Orleans. The push dagger - its crosswise handle making it compact and easy to use-was particularly popular among the Southern gamblers." 5

The push dagger, with the short arrow-head like blade, and crossed handles, looks almost to toy-like to be deadly, as the blade is only about 2 1/2" in length. The deadly thing about a push dagger

Sharp Edges

A push dagger, small enough to be concealed, yet sharp enough to kill a man if used properly. Displayed on the 'Deadman's Hand' aces and eights, the hand Wild Bill Hickok was holding when he was shot. (Author's Collection)

Vannoy
was that, enclosed in the skilled fist of a gambler, the force of the blow would force the knife into the vital organs deeply enough to kill.

Besides the push daggers and bowie knives, gamblers devised several ingenious weapons that were deadly and easily concealed. One such was the knuckle duster, a combination brass knuckles with a short, wicked blade off the end. "In just two swift strokes the user of the short-bladed knuckle-duster could not only smash an antagonist's jaw but also stab him." 6

A good description of a frontier gamblers arsenal is given in the book Doc Holliday, "For a frontier gambler a part of the business of getting dressed for the day consisted in strapping on and tucking away weapons of one sort or another. Some gamblers were asserted to have carried as many as eleven six-shooters, derringers, and knives, racked in tiers from the hideaways in boot tops to the bowie knife dangling down the back of the neck. Doc (Holliday) seems to have carried no more than three weapons, these being a gun in a hip holster worn under the right-hand flap of his jacket, another in a shoulder holster under his left arm and a sheath-knife in his breast pocket." 7

"The professional gambler of the West had to have several perfections. He had to better than good with cards. He had to have a comprehensive knowledge of cheating, for protection against others, as well as for his own use. He had to be swift, accurate, and of sure purpose with a gun. As an emergency precaution, he also had to handy with a sheath-knife." 8

Although on tends to think of gamblers as "flashy dressers," this was usually not the case as in a description of Doc Holliday, "...his clothes were custom made and such as are worn in civilized communities....." 9

In the book, Knights of the Green Cloth, The Saga of the Frontier Gamblers, by Robert K. DeArment, there are several references to knives, although the reference is nearly always to "Bowie Knives," giving us no differentiation between which knives were actually used, although the Bowie knife was undoubtedly one of the more common. One of the queens of the gamblers was a Kitty LeRoy, a young Texas girl who arrived in Deadwood in 1876. One journalist described Kitty as dressing like a gypsy, and she, "had five husband, seven revolvers, a dozen bowie knives, and always went

Sharp Edges

armed to the teeth.... She could throw a bowie knife straighter than any pistol bullet, except her own." 10 It was said that more men were killed in fights over Kitty than over all the other women in the town combined.

Doc Holliday, was often given to using his knife on various occasions. In the book, Doc Holliday, Myers describes Doc's perchance for a knife. Doc, under the name, Tom Mackey, nearly cut off the head of a well-known Denver gambler, Budd Ryan. "The reason for Doc's use of the knife on this occasion was given by Masterson, Earp, and others. Denver, which was already leaving its salad days as a frontier town behind, had strict ordinances against carrying guns, and Doc kept his nose technically clean by only carrying a shiv. Normally, as has elsewhere been stated, he carried his knife in the breast pocket of his jacket, but for better concealment in Denver he is said to have worn it dangling from a lanyard around his neck." 11

Myers goes on to say of Doc, "As he was to prove once more before that year was out, Doc was speedier and deadlier with a knife than most men were with a pistol." he quotes from an article in the San Francisco Weekly Examiner of August 8, 1896. The article was written about some trouble between Holliday and a gent named Ed Bailey. It seems Bailey was trying to cheat, and Holliday called him on it, "Thereupon Bailey started to throw his gun around on Holliday, as might have been expected. But before he could pull the trigger Doc Holliday had jerked a knife out of his breast pocket and with one sideways sweep had caught Bailey just below the brisket." 12

Towns had their share, or sometimes more than their share, of gamblers. In Cheyenne, Wyoming, in 1877, "New saloons and gambling houses opened continually, the madams brought their girls up from Denver by the carload, and the knifings and steel-knucklings were varied by the chin-biting-off and the arrest of a streetwalker......." 13

In 1898 in Skaguay, Alaska, a newspaper clipping reported that "Citizens conferred with the infantry officers, and a week ago today notices were posted warning all concerned that gambling rooms and sure-thing games must be closed and all objectionable characters leave town by 1 o'clock the same day." 14 One of the most

Vannoy

objectionable characters was "Soapy" Smith, who was famous for his gambling and con games.

Gamblers also worked trains and the colorful riverboats of the era. Riverboats and trains, by their very nature, often attracted the Knaves of gambling, as they could skin the passengers, and drop off at the next stop, counting their winnings. Occasionally, they were put off instead. These Knaves, or crooked gamblers, were more often involved with knives, either on the right or wrong end, then were the honest gamblers.

In one instance on a train, two crooked gamblers were working the same train. "The sharper had enticed a group of men around his seat and was loudly announcing his willingness to bet $500 against $250 that he could shuffle the deck and cut the queen of spades with one try." Pat Sheedy, another gambler working the same train, elbowed through the crowd and took the bet, on the condition he be allowed to shuffle the cards. "It was agreed and the stakes were put up. Sheedy riffled the cards and placed the deck face down on the table. The crooked gambler grinned, pulled a knife from beneath his coat, and drove the blade through the deck, saying, "I guess I have cut the queen."

"Show us the queen." Sheedy said. The gambler pulled out the knife and sorted through the deck. The queen was not there. Sheedy had palmed it." _15

Another incident involved Jim Bowie, before he became famous for his part in the invention of the Bowie knife. A son of a friend of Bowie's had taken cotton to Natchez to sell for his father, when he was accosted by a stranger, a "runner" for the gambler, Sturdivant, who was known as one of the foremost gamblers and desperados of Natchez. Young Lattimore, ready to see some city "life" was willing to try his luck, and was quickly fleeced by the gamblers. When his money ran out, he was thrust into the street with orders to "Keep your mouth shut and go home, or in the morning you'll be floating down the river!" Lattimore met up with Bowie, and Bowie gave him some money to play a few more hands. Bowie took over the play after a few rounds, and, when he detected that the dealer was cheating, pocketed the money on the table and prepared to leave. Sturdivant took offense to this, and challenged Bowie to a fight. "Very well," said Bowie, "how will you fight?"

Sharp Edges

Small, easily concealed knives, such as this one, were common weapons of the Old West gamblers. They could be hidden in a sleeve or in the top of a boot. (Author's collection)

Vannoy

The gambler drew a knife and threw it on the table. Bowie did the same. According to legend, they agreed to fight with wrists tied together. "One of the croupiers now took watch in hand, and at his count of "three" the knives clashed. Sturdivant made one stroke, which was parried by Bowie, who then slashed the tendons in his opponent's knife arm." 16 This fight occured before the famous Bowie knife was made, Jim probably used a hunting knife.

In an article from a 1987 Ceaser's World, titled Blackleg Gamblers, magazine, about crooked gamblers, or "Blacklegs" by Ed Dwyer, says, "Absolutely nothing stood in the way of a blackleg intent on "trimming" you, and should dispute erupt, blacklegs would simply murder in cold blood, using ingeniously hidden pistols and daggers." 17

Derringers, palm pistols, and small rimfire pistols were as important to the blacklegs as were the many and varied cheating devices that they carried from game to game, the weaponry backing up the gamblers skill, making sure that he took the pot, one way or another. Many crooked games ended in violence. But to the article by Mr. Dwyer: "Cold steel, too, hurried its share of gamblers to an untimely end. Bowie knives, push knives, daggers, dirks and cane swords provided the blackleg with an additional edge. The Bowie knife was easily the premier knife of it's time, and flush owners would spare no expense on impressive ivory, silver and mother-of-pearl handles and pommels."

"First favored by New Orleans gamblers in the 1840's, the push knife could be easily concealed under the belt, up a sleeve, or in a pocket. Artfully designed French-style doubled-edged daggers with four- to seven- inch blades were always in violent vogue, as were cane daggers and swords that featured ivory pommels and gold mountings. And from France arrived the remarkable three-in-one Apache combination knuckler/dagger/pistol - just the thing for the blackleg who couldn't decide whether to shoot, stab or just beat senseless his opponent." 18

Two of the better known knife makers in San Francisco who marketed these push daggers and other gambling devices were Wills and Finck, and Michael Price.

San Francisco was one of the gambling capitals of the era, and many knife makers abounded in San Francisco. Some of the

Sharp Edges

more notable other than Price, Will & Finck, and Hugh McConnell, were Thomas B. Rogers, John Todt, and Alfred and Jacob H. Schintz.

The gamblers of the west have past into history, like their counterparts, the gold miners, trail hands, and buffalo skinners, but, pieces of their history still remain.

Colorful expressions, still used today, were coined by gamblers during the heyday of the gamblers. "Stacked deck," when the faro dealer prepared a deck with lost of pairs to favor the house,

"Ace up his sleeve," a playing wearing holdout, or gambling device, strapped to the wrist or waist to hold out high cards until needed. "You bet" popularized in San Francisco, is short for, "What do you bet?"

"Passing the buck" refers to the fact that in early poker games the deal would be passed by moving a buckhorn knife from player to player.

So, in our language, and in the collections of museums and private parties, reminiscence of a time when knives were a part of the colorful legacy of the green clothed tables, and the smoky saloons, where the cry of "cheat", could mean a quick grab for a hidden knife, and a man's invitation to his eternal rest.

Afterword

Although *Knives in America's History* covered knives from pre-historic times up until the 1900's, the history of knives keeps going on. In the Spanish American War we see the bowie bayonet for the Krag rifle, the bolo bayonet, the new Hospital Corps knife, and the bolo knife.

In World War I we have the 1917 trench knife, and again, the bolo. In World War II, as airplanes and paratroopers came into use in the Armed Services, the Mark 2 Paratroopers folding knife was issued, and the Mark 3 trench knife, which was an all purpose sheath knife. Later, the Mark 4 bayonet knife was also used. These were mainly issued to combat troops during the wars.

Many soldiers purchased knives privately, and two of these were manufactured by W.D. Randall, Jr., the Model 1 and 2 fighting knife, both of which saw action in the Second World War and the Korean conflict.

Also used was the O.S.S. escape knife, which was a veritable pocket tool kit, consisting of a standard blade, three saw blades, a screw driver, wire cutters, and a can opener.

Although we are a peace today, and the frontier is civilized, knives still capture our imagination. Makers come out with usable and decorative designs, collectors pay large sums for them, and the movies have, once again, brought them into the action via the big screen.

Predator, Rambo, and others again depend on their large, Bowie-type knives to get them out of danger, and thrill those of us in the audience when we think of the lethal value of "Cold Steel."

Sharp Edges

Footnotes

Chapter 1:
1. History of Archery, Edmund Burke, page 174
2. Hunting With a Bow and Arrow, Saxton Pope, pages 23 & 24
3. The Discovery and Conquest of Mexico. Bernal Diaz del Castillo, page 12.
4. World of the American Indian, National Geographic Society, page 274.
5. Firearms, Traps and Tools, Carl P. Russell, page 177, From "Forest and Stream, May 6, 1899, quoted by Woodward: "The Knife." page 11.
6. Journals of Lewis and Clark, Bernard DeVoto, page 222, Houghton Mifflin Company, paperback edition.
7. Ibid, page 226.
8. Firearms, Traps and Tools, page 169
9. Letters and Notes on the Manners, Customs and Condition of the North America Indians, by Geo. Catlin, Vol. 1 page 236
10. Firearms, Traps and Tools, page 182

Chapter 2:
1. Daggers and Fighting Knives, Harold Peterson. page 10
2. Levines Guide to Knives and Their Values, Bernard Levine, page 443
3. Discovery and Conquest of Mexico, Bernal Diaz del Castillo, page 319
4. American Knives, Harold Peterson, page 13
5. Wild Shores, America's Beginnings, Tee Loftin Snell, National Georgaphic Society. page 49
6. Ibid, page 52 7.Ibid, page 53

Vannoy

8 Ibid, page 110 9. Hunting Weapons, Howard L. Blackmore, page 67.

Chapter 3:
1. Master of the Wilderness, Daniel Boone, John Bakless, page 27 page 33, page 36.
2. Firearms, Traps and Tools, Russell, page 168
3. Journals of Lewis and Clark, DeVoto, page 130
4. Journals of the Lewis and Clark Expedition, Vol 2, Gary E. Multon, Editor, page 83
5. Ibid, page 85
6. David Crockett, Crockett, page 378
7. Blade Magazine, Sept/Oct, 1988, Jim Taylor.
8. The American Bowie, It's Origin and Developement. William R. Williamson, Knife Digest, April, 1974
9. Firearms, Traps and Tools, Russell, page 195, taken from Bowie Knife by Raymond Thorp.
10. James Black Legend, William R. Williamson, Blade Magazine, Jan/Feb 1978
11. The James Black Legend, William R. Williamson, in American Blade Magazine, November/Dec. 1977, quoted from American Arms Collector, Vol 1, #3, July 1957, article by Ben Palmer, "The Legend of James Black."
12. Bowie Knife, Raymond Thorp, page 49
13. Ibid, page 32, quoted from American Notes and Queries, March 23, 1889, (II 21) page 251.
14. Blade Magazine, April 1986 Alamo 150 Years Later, J. Bruce Voyles. page 29

Chapter 4
1. Red Dawn at Lexington, Louis Birnbaum, page 84
2. American Knives, Peterson, page 22
3. Collectors Illustrated Encyclopedia of the American Revolution, Neumann and Kravic, page 171
4. Ibid, page 173
5. American Knives, Peterson, page 21
6. Collector's Illustrated Encyclopedia of the American Revolution, Neumann and Kravic, page 161
7. Illustrated History of the Cavalry, Gregory J.W. Urwin, Illustrations: Ernest Lisle Reedstrom, page 46
8. Ibid, page 46

Sharp Edges
9. American Fights and Fighters Series, Revolutionary Fights and Fighters, Cyrus Townsend Brady, LL. D., page 208
10. Ibid page 281
Chapter 5
1. The Beaver Men, Marie Sandoz, page 91
2. Journal of a Mountain Man, James Clyman, edited by Linda Hasselstrom, page ix
3. Across the Wide Missouri, Bernard Devoto, page 43 and 45
4. Firearms, Traps and Tools, Russell, page 180
5. Ibid, page 183
6. Journal of a Mountain Man, Clyman, page 22
10. Lord Grizzly, Frederick Mansfield page
11. Firearms, Traps and Tools, Carl Russell, page 204, from Morgan's Jedediah Smith, pp 239-41
12. Ibid, page 201, from Life in the Far West, Ruxton, U. of Oklahoma Press, 1951, page 189, and Lewis Garrard's Wah-to-Yah and the Taos Trail, U of Oklahoma, 1955, page 163, Orig. published in 1850.
Chapter 6.
1. Journals of Lewis and Clark, DeVoto, page 28
2. Heads, Hides and Horns, Larry Barsness, page 21
3. The Buffalo Book, David Dray, page 129
4. Heads, Hides and Horns, Larry Barsness, page 113
5. Hunting of the Buffalo, E. Douglas Branch, page 168
6. The Buffalo Book, Dray page 103
7. Heads, Hides and Horns, page 120
8. Ibid, page 99
9. Hunting of the Buffalo, Branch, page 159
10. Heads, Hides and Horns, Barsness, page 120
11. Ibid page 99
12. Extermination of the American Bison, Hornaday, page 468
13. Firearms, Traps and Tools, Russell, page 215
14. Bowie Knife, Thorp, page 39
15. The Great Buffalo Hunt Wayne Card, page 47
16. The Buffalo Book, Dray, page 110
17. The Great Buffalo Hunt, Card, page 126
18. Extermination of the American Bison, Hornaday, page 467
19. Ibid, page 442
20. Ibid, page 270

Vannoy

Chapter 7
1. Knifemakers of Old San Francisco, Levine, page 11
2. Time-Life Books, The 49er's, page 79
3. Knifemakers of Old San Franciso, Levine, page 12
4. Time-Life, 49er's page 16
5. American Bowie, Williamson, Knife Digest, April, 1974, page 13
6. Pay Dirt, page 67
7. Gold in them Hills, Strong, page 78-80
8. Knifemakers/Old San Franciso, page 61
9. Alta, (newspaper) Sept 14, 1860, Quoted in Knifemakers, page 62
10. Gold in Them Hills, page 81
11. Ibid, page 82
12. Ibid, page 83
13. American Blade, July/August 1985, Williamson, Bowie Knives
14. American Blade, Sept/Oct 1981 The Mexican Bowie, Vie Walker, page 28.
15. Knifemakers/Old San-Francisco, Levine, page 19
16. Knife Digest, April 1974, American Bowie, Williamson, page 13
17. Prospecting for Gold, From Dogtown to Virginia City, 1852-1864, Granville Stuart, page 74 & 75
18. Pay Dirt, page 132
19. Alaska Sourdough, The Story of Slim Williams, Richard Morenus, page 20
20. Sourdough Saga's, from an 1898 Chicago Tribune Extra, pages 127 & 128
21. Chicago Daily Tribune, March 1898
22. Unabridged Jack London, From the short story, The Son of The Wolf, pages 31, 39 & 40
23. Knifemakers of Old San Francisco, Levine, pages 142 & 143

Chapter 9
1. Military Dress of North American, page 74, plate #49
2. Charleston Mercury, Feb. 1862
3. Illustrated History of the Cavalry, page 114
4. Civil War Collectors Encyclopedia, Francis Lord, page 151
5. Ibid, page 152
6. American Civil War, Earl Schenck Miers, page 60
7. Levines Guide to Knives and Their Values, page 317
8. Confederate Arms, Albaugh and Simmons, page 123

Sharp Edges
9. Levines Guide, page 317
10. Confederate Arms, page 232-237, 223-228
11. The Blue and The Grey, Commager, page 337
12. U.S. Cavalry, an Illustrated History, Urwin, page 114
13. Blade Magazine, August, 1988 Edges of the Past
14. Confederate Arms, page 124
15. Letter from Jimmy Lile, "The Arkansas Knifesmith."
17. Blade Magazine, June 1986 Clink, Clash and Glitter of Steel, Austerman
18. Bowie Knife, Thorp page 67 & 68
18. Blue and the Grey, Commager, page 337
20. Blade Magazine. Williamson, American Bowie, Newspaper, The Slavesv Friend
21 Blue and the Grey, Commager, page 279
22. Ibid, page 279
23. American Civil War, page 248
24. Blade June 1986, Austerman
25. Blue and The Grey, Commager, page 1024
26. Article in the Arkansas Quarterly, by Leo Huff, from a letter sent to me by the Arkansas Historical Society.
27. Confederate Arms, Albaugh and Simmons, page 121
28. The Blue and The Grey, Commager, page 870
29. Ibid, page 979.
30. Ibid, page 790
31. Ibid, page 790
32. American Knives, Petersen, page 31

Chapter 9.
1. Military Life in the Dakotas, Regis de Trobriand, page 64
2. Ibid page 49
3. 40 Miles a Day on Beans and Hay, page 258, Interview with George App, Third Infantry, 1873-78, in the Bridgeport, Conn. Post, July 27, 1933
4. American Knives, Petersen, page 71
5. Man at Arms Magazine, NRA publication, July/Aug 1980
6. Firearms, Traps and Tools, Russell, page
7. Beans and Hay, page 268
8. Illustrated History of the Cavalry, page 150
9. Bugles, Banners and Warbonnets, page 191

Vannoy
10. Time-Life Books, The Soldiers, page 110
11. Bugles, Banners, and Warbonnets, page 264
12. Ibid
13. Ibid, 256.
14. Lakota Recollections of the Custer Fight, New Sources of Indian-Military History. Edited by Richard G. Hardorff. 1991 Arthur H. Clark Company, Spokane, Wash. 1997 edition University of Nebraska Press, Lincoln, Nebraska. page 101.
15. I fought with Custer, The Story of Sergeant Windolph, Last Survivor of the Battle of the Little Big Horn as told to Frazier and Robert Hunt. 1947. Bison Books Edition 1987, University of Nebraska Pres, Lincoln, Neb. page 103
16. ibid. page 92
17. Lakota Recollections, page 84
18. ibid page 65
19. ibid, page 32, Respects Nothing Interview.
20. ibid, page 94
21. Guns of the Gunfighters, Guns and Ammo Magazine publication, page 162

Chapter 10.
1. Bowie Knife, Thorp, page 38
2. Time-Life Books, The Cowboys, page 54
3. The West that Was, Leaky page 114 & 115
4. Monte Walsh, Jack Shaffer, 383 & 383
5. Ride the Dark Trail, Louis L'Amour, page 52 & 53
6. Log of a Cowboy, Andy Adams, page 94
7. Cowboy Culture, page 157
8. Old Time Cowhand, Raymond Adams, page 259
9. Knives, '86, Ken Warner, page 160
10. West that Was, Leaky, page 163

Chapter 11.
1. Book of Knives, Yvan A. Deviaz, page 61
2. Knifemakers/Old San Francisco, Levine page 39
3. Ibid page 98
4. Time-Life Books, The Gamblers, page 142
5. Ibid page 142

Sharp Edges
6. Doc Holliday, John Myers Myers, page 48
7. Ibid, page 37
8. Doc Holliday, page 241
9. Knights of the Green Cloth, page 253
10. Doc Holliday, page 57
11. Ibid, page 68
12. Chicago Daily Tribune, March, .1889
13. Green Cloth, page 321
14. Bowie Knife, Thorp, page 129-131
17. Ceasers World, Jan/Feb. 1987, BlackLeg Gamblers, Ed Dwyer, with Thanks the William Williamson.
21. ibid
22. ibid

Vannoy
Other source materials
The American Heritage Picture History of the Civil War Editor Richard M. Ketchum, 1960, American Heritage Publishing, Doubleday Books, NY
Red Dawn at Lexington, Louis Birnbaum, Houghton Mifflin, Boston, 1986
Daggers and Fighting Knives of the Western World, Stone Age till 1900, Harold L. Peterson, Walker and Company, NY 1968
The Book of Knives, Yvan A. de Riaz, Crown Publishers, NY 1978 Doc Holliday, John Myers Myers, Bison Book, U of Nebraska, 1955
The American Civil War, Earl Schenck Miers, Ridge Press/Golden Press, NY 1961
Levine's Guide to Knives and their values, Bernard Levine,
American Knives, Harold Peterson, 1958, Gun Room Press, Highland Park, NJ Reprint edition, 1980.
History of Knives, Harold Peterson, 1966 Charles Scribner's Sons, NY.
American's Fascinating Indian Heritage, Readers Digest, Pleasantville, NY.
World of the American Indian, National Geographic Society, 1974, Washington, DC
American Heritage Book of Indians, 1961, American Heritage Publishing Co.
Plains Indians, Thomas E. Mails, Bonanza Books, NY 1973
Knives '86, Ken Warner, 1986, DBI Books, 111
Hunting With a Bow and Arrow, Saxton Pope, 1923 G.P. Putman's Sons.
Piltdown Productions brochure on modern day obsidian tools.
History of Archery, 1957, Edmund Burke, William Morrow and Company
The Blue and the Grey, Henry Steele Commager, 1982, Fairfax Press, Bobbs - Merrill Company.
The Dawn's Early Light, Walter Lord, 1972, W.W. Norton and Company, Inc. New York
Civil War Days, John Bowen, Chartwell Books, Inc. 1987 The Coming Fury, Bruce Catton, Doubleday and Company, 1961
Pictorial History of the U.S. Army, Gene Gurney, Crown Publishers, NY 1977
The U. S. Cavalry, An Illustrated History, Gregory Urwin, Blandford Press, NY 1983

Sharp Edges

Military Dress of North America, Martin Windrow and Gerry Embleston, 1973, Iam Alien, LTD, London.

Hunting Weapons Howard L. Blackmore, Walker and Co, NY 1971

Confederate Arms, William A. Albaugh III and Edward N. Simmons, Bonanza Books, NY 1957

Master of the Wilderness Daniel Boone: John Bakless. William Morrow and Company, NY 1939

Daniel Boone, The pioneer of Kentucky: John S.C. Abbott, Dodd Mead and Company, NY 1941

Captian Paul: Commander Edward Elliberg, Dodd, Mead and Company, NY 1941

Daniel Boone, Wilderness Scout: Stewart Edward White, Doubleday, Doran and Company, Inc. Garden City, NY 1936

The Discovery of North America. WP Gumming, R.A. Skelton, D.B Quinn, American Heritage Press, NY 1972

The Life of David Crockett: Autobiogroaphy, David Crockett, A.L. Burt Company, publishers, NY 1902

Sourdough Sagas Edited by Berbertt L. Heller, The World Publishing Company, NY 1967

James Bowie and his Famous Knife: Shannon Garst, Julian Messner, Inc. NY 1955.

The Navel Officer's Sword: Captain Henry T. A. Bosanquet, Her Majesty's Stationary Office, London, 1955

Pay Dirt, Glenn Chesney Quiett, D. Appleton-Century Company, Inc. New York - London, 1936. (page66, Welsh miners looking mean.) Page 132, (dug and panned gold until my belt knife wore out.) page 212, dying of starvation, Rose.

Gold in Them Hills, Being an Irreverent History of the Great 1849 Gold Rush, Phil Strong, Doubleday and Company, NY 1957

Journals of the Lewis and Clark Expedition, Volume 2, August 30, 1803 - August 4, 1804, Gary E. Moulton, editor, University of Nebraska, 1986. Page 445, man went back for knife page 83 rain got supplies wet.

Journals of Lewis and Clark, Bernard Devoto Houghton Mifflin Company, Boston. 1953 page 130

Firearms, Traps and Tools of the Mountain Men, Carl P. Russell, University of New Mexico Press, Albuquerque. 1967

Time-Life Books, Time-Life Books, New York. The Old West Seris, Series Editor, Ezra Bowen. The Cowboys, 1973, Time, Inc. Text: William H. Forbis, The Soldiers, The Forty-Niners, The Gamblers, The Alaskans, The Miners,

Vannoy
Bowie Knife, Raymond W. Thorp, U of New Mexico Press, Albuquerque, 1948
The West that Was, John Leakey, As told to Nellie Snyder Yost, U of Nebraska Press, Lincoln and London, 1965
Various Blade Magazines with articles of my own on various subjects covered in the book.
Blade, November/Dec 1986, Buffalo Skinner Knives, March/April 1987, Knives of the Cowboys, July/August 1987, Knives of the Indians, Sept/Oct 1988, Knives of the Gamblers, Nov/Dec 1987, Knives of the Mountain Men, May/June 1988, Knives of the Frontier Cavalry.
Also other articles in Blade magazines: June 1986, Clank, Clash and Glitter of Steel, Part 1, Bowies and Bayonets, Wayne R. Austerman. Mexican Bowies, Oct. 1981, Vie Walker. The Spanish Notch, by William R. Williamson, July/August, 1975 The James Black Legend, Parts 1 and 2, William R. Williamson, Nov/Dec. 1977, Jan/Feb 1978, Alamo, 150 Years,
Man at Arms, NRA Publications, July/August, 1980 Dragoons and Sabres, The Savage Recessional, 1850-1942, Wayne R. Austerm

www.ingramcontent.com/pod-product-compliance
Lightning Source LLC
Chambersburg PA
CBHW070452090426
42735CB00012B/2521